Phases of Childhoo

Bernard Lievegoed

Phases of Childhood

Floris Books
Anthroposophic Press

Translated by Tony Langham and Plym Peters

First published in Dutch in 1946 under the title
Ontwikkelingsfasen van het kind
by Uitgeverij Vrij Geestesleven, Zeist.
Translated from the eighth edition of 1985.
First published in English in 1987.
© Copyright 1985 Uitgeverij Vrij Geestesleven, Zeist
This translation © Floris Books, Edinburgh, 1987.

Published in the United Kingdom by Floris Books,
21 Napier Road, Edinburgh EH10 5AZ.
Published in the United States by Anthroposophic Press, Inc.
Bell's Pond, Star Route, Hudson, NY 12534.

British Library CIP Data available

ISBN 0-86315-066-7 (Floris Books)

ISBN 0-88010-189-X (Anthroposophic Press)

Printed in Great Britain
by Billing & Sons, Worcester

Contents

Preface

Anyone critically re-reading a book he wrote himself many years ago, during the Second World War, finds himself in an unenviable position, and should, in fact, rewrite the whole thing. Science has not stood still in the meantime and other interests have become central in his own development.

Re-reading this book brings back the reality of the war years when life was lived very intensely; when we were groping to find a way of building a better world 'later'.

This building of the unknown future was characteristic of the Waldorf (Rudolf Steiner) School movement in clandestine training courses for young people, hiding from the Germans, and aiming to become teachers later on.

This book about the developmental stages of childhood was the result of a course I gave for these young people at that time. I have no time to rewrite the book, and any attempt to update it fully would also lead to rewriting it. It is therefore republished, with minimum revision, where material is still relevant, at the request of young parents and teachers today.

What *has* changed is the child's environment and the measure of freedom given children and young people, to enable them to find their way.

The understanding supervision of adults is important for this to take place.

B.C.J. Lievegoed

Introduction

Every school of psychology and pedagogy is based on a certain philosophy and particular *a priori* assumptions. This is true even when such a background is denied.

Psychology as the science of the psyche, the human soul, depends on what is understood by the psyche or soul.

Pedagogy is determined by a view of mankind and what people are to be educated to become. The concept of soul has been interpreted in totally different ways in different cultures, periods of history and movements, depending on whether the prevailing attitudes were based on theology, philosophy or the natural sciences. At the end of the nineteenth century there was even a period of a soul-less psychology. Today 'scientific' psychology again depends on the psychologist's own school or movement. The fact is that in psychological research the only answers to be found are those to the questions raised *a priori* (either consciously or *unconsciously*).

This apples to an even greater extent in pedagogy. For a teacher is not merely a curious observer, but an active person, and the direction and content of his activity is determined by the goal he has set himself.

This goal is the adult who will have to transmit and continue culture into the society of future decades. For this reason each cultural period had its own pedagogic ideal.

For the Greeks the ideal was a gymnast; not a

muscle man, but someone who had developed harmoniously both physically and spiritually, so that the body could serve entirely as an instrument of the spirit.

Greek educations took place in the *palaestra* by means of gymnastics, and to a corresponding extent in the *orchestra*, the dancing places where Greek youths performed rhythmic dances to music and learned to express certain spiritual values in gestures. Plato even declared that the state should be organized on the basis of music: the better the music, the better the state it would produce. For the Arcadians, music was an obligatory subject up to the age of thirty.

The educational ideal of the Romans was the rhetor, a master of rhetoric, who could convince others with his arguments and thus help to lead the state. The Roman educational ideal was of a practical, political nature and the state was the most important creation of the citizens.

From the late Middle Ages to the present day, the ideal has been the professor, someone who is very knowledgeable: 'Knowledge is power'.

During the nineteenth century when the scientific revolution permeated every aspect of life, even psychology and pedagogy did not escape its influence.

The Darwinian theory of evolution was held consistently and led to the ideal of man as a soldier, 'the survival of the fittest'. Pedagogy served this ideal.

A 'practical ideal' resulting from industrialization was the emergence of the 'specialist'. Education must provide for specialization at the earliest possible stage, avoiding any trimmings, to meet this ideal 'production line' person, who is actually a cog in the complicated economic machinery.

This materialist view of the individual results in the gathering of as much knowledge as possible, because knowledge equals power, not because knowledge can lead to wisdom.

Pedagogy today is also a result of the predominant schools of thought, and those who are not directly concerned with education and who simply send their children to school are in tacit agreement with the educational ideal of the last century.

However, our fight about schooling proves that parents certainly wish their children to be educated to the ideal which they hold themselves. A neutral, Protestant or Catholic education will have a different influence and instil different ideals because the teachers will exert a different influence on the children.

However, the struggle over education is not necessarily concerned with the *content* of the syllabus, but with the widely- held view from the nineteenth century, that the child is a *tabula rasa,* and that children should acquire a certain body of knowledge in the most efficient manner possible. The whole curriculum has a very materialistic-individual character.

The ideal that man should be educated to be a harmonious person, on the one hand developing *practical skills,* on the other hand becoming a bearer of *beauty, wisdom and culture,* does not play any, or only a very small part in this. To effect a change the entire curriculum would have to be based on completely different principles.

With different schools defining the same terms differently or ascribing a very particular meaning to certain words, it is essential to outline briefly the philosophy on which this work is based and what is meant by some words, such as the soul, and the spirit.

The ideas about the development of the child which

11

are put forward here are in line with the Goethean viewpoint developed by Rudolf Steiner in the field of education in the twentieth century. Rudolf Steiner himself never created a systematic school of psychology. In the six years between 1919 and 1925 when he was still able to elaborate his theories on education, he limited himself to general pedagogy in discussion with teachers and in his own lectures.

In this introduction we will only deal very briefly with his main starting points, concentrating only on what is necessary for understanding the rest of this book.

Man is *not* a creature who is born in only a physical sense, developing certain spiritual characteristics from this physical body which are predetermined by hereditary factors. Man is a being participating in two worlds, a material-physical world, as well as a divine-spiritual world.

A child comes into the world with an inherited body *and* with a spiritual individuality (entelechy), a spiritual being with its own spiritual structure. This statement is based on different *a priori* views from those of the Lockean tradition, which holds that the entire development of life is determined solely by genetic potential and the influence of the environment.

The assumptions for this book are that in human physical and spiritual development there is both a genetic and a biographical potential. The latter is revealed in consciousness as our 'self', the deepest core of our being.

The self is felt as a reality in the psyche, the human soul.

Drives and needs arise from physical aspects seeking fulfilment. They enter the soul and are felt there. Thus the human soul receives stimuli and gains its content from two sources: firstly, from the physical

12

world through basic drives and the senses; secondly, from the spiritual world through the self. The spirit (self) and matter (body) meet in an intermediate area, the human soul. This middle area alone forms the object of the study of psychology.

This can be summarized in the following schematic diagram:

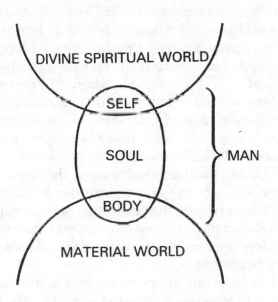

In this the self, the individual is a part, a structure of the divine spiritual world and the body is a part, a structure of the material world.

Thus man is seen as threefold, with a body, a soul and a spirit.

What is meant here by spirit should become clear from this description.

The concept of the soul, as the object of study of psychology differs in its meaning from the dualistic interpretation of body and soul.

In his *On the Aesthetic Education of Man* Schiller founded his psychology on a tripartite view of man. He distinguished a 'spiritual drive', the individual principle of self, in the soul, also known as *Formtrieb*, and a *Stoff* or *Sachtrieb*, the drives and needs arising from the physical body. Between these the creative man unfolds through his real soul-element: the urge to play, *Spieltrieb*.

During the past century psychology has been almost exclusively concerned with the effects of the physical parts of man on his soul. It was either a sensory psychology (the entire nineteenth century) or a psychology based on needs (psychoanalysis, individual psychology). Many important facts became clear as a result and occasionally there are glimpses of a study of the individual, combining principle as in *Gestalt* psychology and the schools concerned with morality.

This book will attempt to study the development of the child from the above-mentioned points of view. We are convinced that there can only be happy, wise and skilled people when education takes into account the development of the body, spirit and soul, from the very beginning.

The following chapters are summaries of lectures and courses given during the war years for interested parents and young teachers. The book that has emerged from these is aimed at similar readers. There are not very many references; the professional will recognize which ideas form part of the body of modern psychology and when new ideas are being developed. For the untrained constant interruptions in the text referring to the opinion of others can become unnecessarily tedious.

1. The three cycles of development

Developmental psychology covers an extremely wide field which can be approached an illuminated from many different angles. In a work of this sort that is obviously impossible, and the aim is therefore to concentrate on particular aspects of the psychological development of children, and to order the facts in their organic relationships.

The following chapters describe the physical and mental stages of development. For the soul development, the starting point has been the relationship of the child with the world around him.

The second half of the book then deals with problems which are of special importance for education, from the points of view which have emerged in the first half.

A survey of the development of the child from newborn baby to adulthood at the age of twenty-one reveals three distinct major periods: the first baby-and-toddler phase when the child is still entirely surrounded by the parental home and when he is still entirely 'under mother's wing'; a second phase, when he takes a step further into the world, and school as well as home becomes a part of his life; and a third phase, following the primary school period, which is devoted to preparing for a future career.

From a biological point of view the same periods can again be distinguished. First, the period from birth to the change of teeth; secondly, the period from this point up to puberty; thirdly, that from puberty to adulthood.

These can be taken as three periods of about seven years each.

Obviously a different emphasis can be discerned in individual developments and between boys and girls. These differences will be more fully discussed in what follows, nevertheless the three major periods can be considered to be a general average.

We continue with a broad description of the relationship of the child with the world around him in these three periods.

The small child is characterized by a great openness to the outer world. He assimilates everything in his environment without any special resistance and meets the world with unlimited trust. He lives in paradisal innocence in a world where good and evil are inextricably interwoven.

All the senses are open and the child answers with inner activity expressed in imitation or mimicry. He (or she) learns to speak through imitation, and in this way the door to human spirituality is opened for him. Through imitation he will learn all the useful and negative things which characterize the interaction of human beings. The basis for future morality is also laid down by a more subtle imitation.

The fact that, on the other hand, the child is himself creative at an early age does not contradict this view, but his relationship to the world around him is based on a trust and openness that is no longer possible at any other stage of life. The difference becomes apparent when comparing a three-year-old toddler with a child in the middle of the second developmental stage. By about nine, a child already has his own little world in which he lives. This is rather like a fairy-tale

16

garden, surrounded by a high wall, shutting him off from the real world.

In his own kingdom the child is king, and just as in fairy-tales, anything he dreams up is possible. Within the safe walls he plants the flowers in the fairy-tale garden which can grow into all sorts of marvellous plants. The outside world only penetrates in a fragmented way and the elements from outside are taken up into his own world and altered until they fit into it. The child has many friends at this stage; he seeks company, though the friendships formed during this period are still rather superficial. They are not deep and are determined by the need to live and play in his own world with others.

The child is happy in himself and only becomes unhappy when impressions enter from outside which cannot be assimilated. They intrude violently and he finds no place for them. These impressions are then either isolated and surrounded with a little wall, or they are transformed after a time and finally assimilated in an unexpected way. In the first case, there is an unassimilated chunk of experience which can result in disturbances in soul life later on.

It is only in the third period, with the onset of puberty, that these walls are broken down and gradually begin to crumble. Only now is the teenager again brought face to face with naked reality. He wishes to conquer this from within and is able to do so because he has achieved a spiritual unity during the previous period. In his own world he has discovered a centre, and everything is related to this or springs from it: the child's own self. From this centre he penetrates the outside world and tries to adapt it to his own norms; he has become socially active. The friendships

17

formed at this stage are genuine, where other persons are sought as individuals.

This can be illustrated schematically with the following diagram:

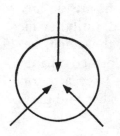 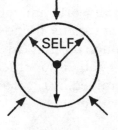 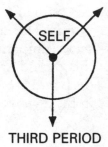

FIRST PERIOD   SECOND PERIOD   THIRD PERIOD

This outline attempts to illustrate the following idea.

In the first period the most important relationship with the outside world is from outside inwards. However, the experiences which result from this are not initially assimilated into the centre of the self. During the second period the child is an enclosed unit. Forces emanate from the centre of the self to the periphery. The outside world does not penetrate unhindered, it merely makes an impression at the boundary and is assimilated only after a 'digestive' process. During the third period the main direction is from the inside outwards. There is an attempt to conquer and alter the outside world. It is only in the years after reaching adulthood that this one-sided direction of activity achieves a balance, because the outside world once again penetrates inwards and the

18

adult becomes open to it. This provides the experiences of life.

Thus the fourth stage could be described as the adult balance, in which activity moving outwards alternates with experiences coming in from outside.

FOURTH PERIOD   FIFTH PERIOD

However, this fourth stage is only achieved in adult life and through adult experience, and therefore does not belong in a discussion of the development of the child.

It would even be possible to add a fifth stage to the diagram in which activity outwards gradually decreases until in old age a person lives in the memory of what was assimilated earlier. This results in a condition of contemplative wisdom which is a characteristic of a healthy old person. It bears a great similarity to that of the small child; the main difference is that the outside world is now compressed within the focus of the self.

A survey of these five possible developmental stages reveals that there is a certain equilibrium in both the second and fourth periods. These two stages are related, and it will be seen that the second stage, in particular, is a preparation for the long fourth stage.

This second stage is a bugbear of child psychologists. A survey of the literature on the first stage and on puberty and the years following puberty shows that very little attention has been paid to the intervening years. In analytical psychology this period of equilibrium has sometimes been called the latent period. Because of its enclosed character and inner equilibrium it seems to be of little interest and lacking in striking features. Indeed, for this period a different method of research should be used. Experimental psychology has also come up against an impenetrable wall around the child during this period, although it has shed so much light on interesting aspects of the first period. Only educational psychology has been concerned with processing the facts which were collected by others.

During the third period the young person can express himself again and the outside world can discover what is happening in his soul during and after puberty. However, this certainly does not mean that development during this latent period is any less important than that in the previous or following periods.

The three main stages were roughly outlined above. At the end of each period elements of the following period can be found, and the child is already preparing for this. Thus there is a transition period from the toddler to the school-age child, and a pre-puberty period when the puberty stage can already be detected. This will be discussed in greater detail in the following chapters.

Up to now, the point of view has been social. But again, using the young child as a starting point, the three periods can be characterized in a slightly different way: during the first period the child is mainly interested in imitation; the second period is a time of emotional development, while the third is a time of ideas.

Every psychologist concerned with the laws governing child development will arrive at a particular division of stages. These differ because each starts from a different viewpoint and is therefore investigating other functions. The various divisions are usually correct from the viewpoint chosen, but they are incomplete and there is no overall summary which clearly explains how these theories can be united in a greater whole.

For this reason an attempt has been made in this work to deal with development from many different viewpoints, and to compare the resulting schemes. To study the relationship between inner and outer world produces a division into the seven-year periods which coincide with biological development. If the functions of thought, feeling and the will are examined separately, different stages emerge and the same also applies in examining the development of the self and the memory.

It is only if all these aspects are combined that there is a synthesis in which reciprocal influences can be shown and which finally leads to a flexible view comparable to a film of plant-growth over a number of months seen in a few minutes. Leaf after leaf can be seen unfurling, one can observe periods of rapid and slow growth, the arrival of the bud and the blossom.

We should be able to build up this sort of view of child development in our mind's eye, so that we can watch progress, not only as regards physical growth, but also the development of the psyche.

If we wish to form a complete picture, for example, of the eighth year, we can ask such questions as: at

21

what stage of physical development is an eight-years-old child? At what stage are the thought processes, the feelings and the will, and how far has the self developed? It is only then that the appropriate educational measures and the correct teaching materials can be found. It will also be possible to ascertain to what extent intuitive educational measures have been correct.

2. The physical stages of development

The division of child development from infancy to adulthood into three main periods, each approximately seven years long, was based on psychological development.

First, we should like to discover to what extent these periods have also a physical basis, as evident in the child's changing figure.

The changes which occur during puberty are sufficiently well-known in broad terms; the changes at the age of seven are usually only characterized by the loss of milk teeth, although this is actually only part of the physical changes taking place at the age of seven.

Zeller described the changes in the child's figure at this age in great detail, illustrating his description with a wonderful collection of photographs, some of which are shown in this chapter. Above all, Zeller pointed out the great importance of the seventh year of life when physical changes take place which are as radical as those of puberty.

Since Stratz carried out his pioneering studies of the growth of children, it has been recognized that the physical development occurs in rhythmic stages in which the stretching of the limbs alternates with a filling-out in breadth. During these periods the interrelationship of parts of the body changes considerably.

The ratios of physical measurements are known

particularly to artists. In the average adult the head is 1:7 to 1:8 of the total body length.

The classical ratio is considered to be 1:8, which is the ratio generally found in people 1.80 m (6 feet) tall.

Smaller people have a slightly lower ratio. However, the ratio of head to body in a baby is 1:4; the head accounts for a quarter of the total length.

These ratios can be seen in Stratz's well-known diagram (Figure 1). He distinguished the following periods:

First developmental period: 0 - 7 years
1.   0 - 1:   baby
2.   2 - 4:   first growth in breadth (toddler)
3.   5 - 7:   first growth in length (school age child)

Second developmental period of the child: 8 - 20 years
4.   8 - 10:   second growth in breadth
5.   11 -15:   second growth in length (girls: 11 - 14, boys 13 - 15)
6.   15 - 20:   maturity (third growth in breadth).

We shall return later to Stratz's diagram, which gives the ratios of 4, 5, 6, 7 and 8 head lengths. The changes in figure can be described even more precisely than in Stratz's scheme, and to some extent Zeller did this. He distinguished three stages during the first seven years, each with its own characteristic figure. They could be called the baby figure, the toddler figure and the transitional figure. Normally a child reaches the figure of a school age child by the age of seven.

The second period starts with this school-age figure, which is transformed in breadth between the ages of

Head:body ratio

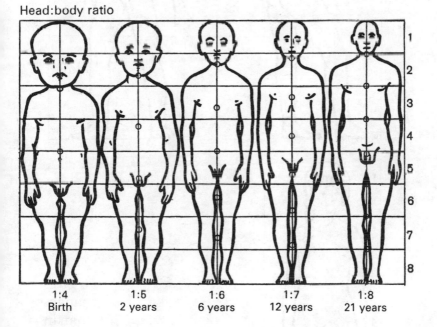

| 1:4 | 1:5 | 1:6 | 1:7 | 1:8 |
| Birth | 2 years | 6 years | 12 years | 21 years |

Figure 1. Scheme of body proportions according to Stratz.

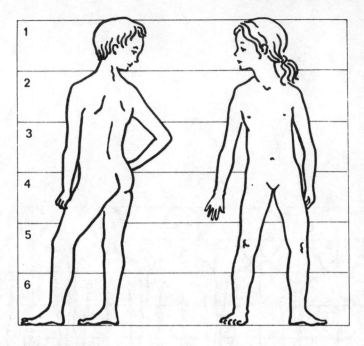

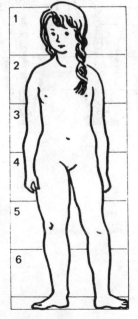

*Figure 2. Boy and girl, aged seven.
With the boy the S-shape of the
spine can clearly be seen.*

*Figure 3. Age eight. Beginning
of the second growth in breadth.
Ratio of head to length 1:6.25.*

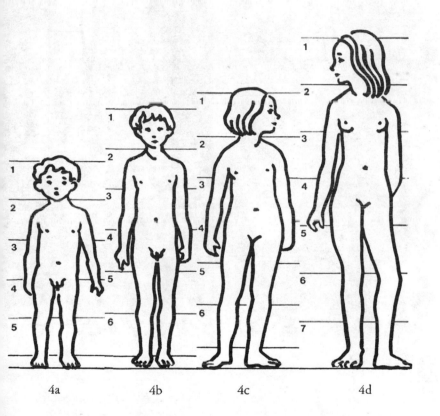

Figure 4. Normal development according to Geyer.
  a First growth in breadth (nursery-schoolchild)
  b First growth in height (schoolchild, age 7).
  c Second growth in breadth (age 9).
  d Second growth in length (pubescent, age 12).

27

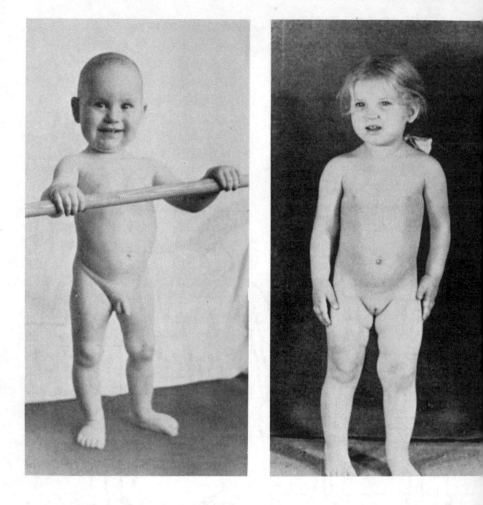

Figure 5. Age one.   Figure 6. Age 2 years 8 months.

eight and ten, when a new figure emerges towards puberty.

The third period begins with the pubescent figure, which is followed by the third period of growth in breadth, and then the figure reaches maturity. This process finishes at the age of eighteen when the young man or woman slowly continues to develop towards an adult figure.

It is immediately noticeable that these meta- morphoses in the figure coincide with the periods of psychological development.

We shall attempt to describe these various periods in the development of the human form and clarify this with some illustrations.

2.1 The baby

The large head is a characteristic feature of a baby's figure; the distance from chin to crown is a quarter of the total body length. The same distance again brings it to the navel. The relatively enormous size of the head is only really apparent when one imagines it enlarged to adult size. A baby cannot touch its fingertips above its head with stretched arms.

The line through the eyes is considerably below the middle of the head. In other words, the size of the skull is quite a bit larger than the facial area. The bottom half of the face, the lower jaw, is small and receding, the middle part of the face relatively developed, although the nose barely protrudes but the great domed forehead is enormous and impressive. The eyes are large and the iris accounts for a large part of the visible eye. The top edge of the ear is on a level with the line through the pupils so that the ears are placed low down on the head.

The features are still rounded and soft, the mouth pouts with a small bubble on the upper lip — the result

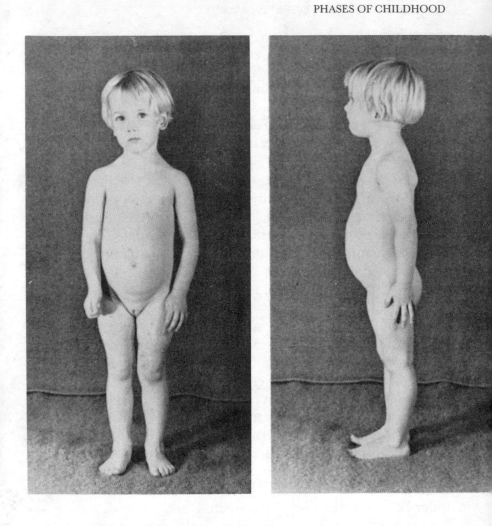

Figures 7 and 8. Age 3 years 4 months.

of sucking. The head is as broad as the whole chest, which is still cylindrical and shapeless, passing straight into the baby's tummy. The pectoral girdle is broader that the pelvic girdle, as any midwife knows. The arms are short and more or less follow the growth of the trunk so that they lie approximately on the hips. The pelvis and legs are relatively the least developed. the legs are only one and a half times the length of the head (inconceivable in an adult). They are round with characteristic folds on the insides of the thighs.

Thus the upper half of the body runs ahead of the lower half: the head in relation to the trunk, the shoulders in relation to the pelvis, the skull in relation to the facial structure, the eye sockets in relation to the lower jaw, and so on.

The actual lack of a neck is characteristic of the baby figure. The round head seems to be directly placed in the trunk with only a few folds between the two.

The skin of a healthy baby is stretched over the fatty pads. The joints are strongly indented as though there is an elastic band around them. The muscles are not yet developed and are not visible through the skin.

This baby figure lasts more or less for the first one and a half years. During the second year there is a shift in growth and the lower parts of the body start to develop more, reducing the proportional size of the upper half.

2.2 The toddler

When this happens, the pattern changes. The child now has quite different proportions, and is usually described as a toddler figure. This figure remains as a basic pattern from tow and a half to five years of age.

The ratio of the head to the body length is 1:5, instead of 1:4, as in the baby. Thus the body has grown more quickly than the head, although this has also

31

increased in size. The relatively greater length of the body is due mainly to the growth of the trunk. Usually the trunk of a toddler has increased in length more than the legs, though in some cases they grow at the same rate, and are of the same length. However, as yet there is no sign of strong growth in the legs.

Because of this growth of the trunk, especially in breadth (first period of growth in breadth), the large stomach is a characteristic feature of the toddler, just as the head was for the baby.

The trunk is cylindrical, the back is still straight and there is no sign yet of the S-shaped curve of the spine so characteristic of later years. The stomach is fat, with a clear semi-circular fold underneath. The chest opens downwards into the stomach without any clear demarcation; the child does not yet have a waist. The angle of the ribs at the bottom is still flat, and the pelvis is now as broad as the shoulders.

In comparison with that of a baby, the child's neck has emerged slightly, but the head still sits just on the shoulders.

The skin is still shaped by subcutaneous fat and the muscles do not show. However, the folds in the thighs disappear, as do the pads on the hands and feet. The joints are in line with the limbs, the indentations having disappeared.

The head is relatively smaller, as shown by the ratio given above of 1:5. The eyes are still below the halfway mark, so that the large forehead still predominates.

However, the chin has come forward slightly so that the face has more expression. Nevertheless, the upper lip still protrudes above the lower, the features are still soft and formless. The eyes look out trustfully on the world ready to react to it with joy or rejection.

The limbs are rounded and thicker. The movements have the same rounded character, they are not yet purposeful and therefore angular. The illustration shows a normal toddler at the age of three (Figures 6, 7, 8).

2.3 Ready for school

At about the age of five the toddler's figure starts to change dramatically. These are the years of the first growth in length, which is largely concentrated in the legs.

While the child still has a toddler's facial features and the characteristic abdomen the limbs start to grow longer and more slender. The padded surface disappears and the muscles become visible, the joints appear as separate parts. The knees, in particular, become more flexible. The patella is now visible and the broad ends of the bones of the leg are noticeable.

The nose, though still small, is slightly more in evidence, the upper lip still protrudes above the lower lip.

This is the age at which the child is ready for school and when his play changes and becomes more purposeful, as will be described later.

The child's movements too become angular and purposeful. He becomes very agile and he walks in quite a different way. Instead of toddling along he now takes real steps. Especially when he runs there is a great difference.

Gradually the trunk becomes slimmer and starts to divide into two parts. The waist develops, dividing the stomach from the chest as the latter narrows lower down; the angle of the ribs becomes more pronounced, the breast bone recedes between the pectoral muscles. The stomach grows flat and the semi-circular fold below it is less pronounced. The spinal column takes on S-shaped curvature and becomes more graceful. The pectoral girdle becomes broader and more flexible. The collar bones become more pronounced and hollows form making the upper arm-bones stand out. The shoulder blades become more prominent on the back and the neck grows longer, giving the head greater freedom of movement.

Zeller describes this transformation as follows: 'The figure of the school-age child can be qualitatively compared with that of the toddler. It cannot be reconstructed by dimensional changes — the changes include the entire psycho-physical personality. The main aspect of the new physical structure is in the predominance of motor functions.'

2.4 School age

At about the age of seven the face also starts to change markedly. By this time the school-age figure has developed and the child enters the second major stage.

The head grows even less in comparison with the rest of the body and the ratio is now 1:6. The eyes are now above the halfway line so that the forehead is less dominant — the eyes have become smaller and have a different expression; they are more expectant, conscious and critical. The upper lip no longer protrudes above the lower lip and the mouth is thinner, tighter and less open.

The whole impression is one of slim agility and easy, comfortable mobility, of an elegance which was lacking in the toddler. Very often children are rather thin and owing to their growth in length have insufficient weight for other growth. The child now enters a completely new stage of life.

The toddler was entirely at home in the protected environment of the parental nest where his helplessness was sheltered by the mother. The school-

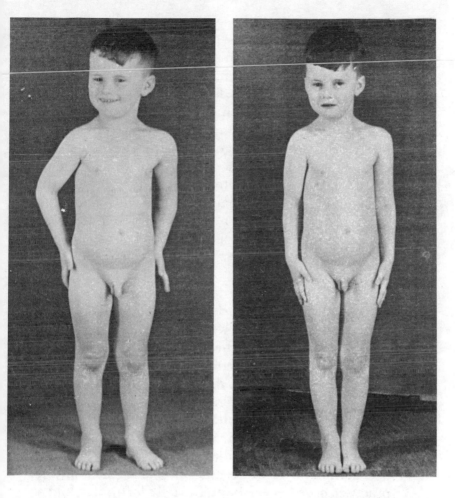

Following pages show the same boy between the age of 4 years 7 months, and 16 years 8 months.

Figure 9. Age 4 years 7 months

Figure 10. Age 5 years 8 months.

age child has freed himself from this limited world, both physically and psychologically. He can now enter the wide world on his own two legs, horizons are broadened and a certain degree of independence shows in his movements, figure and facial expression.

This psychological change is very important in regard to a child's readiness for school. He is only ready for school when this transformation to independence is expressed in physical development. It is often clear that children who still bear the traits of the toddler stage are unable to cope with school life and find the first years very difficult, not so much from the academic, as from the social point of view. They cannot mix with others, are teased and feel very miserable.

Besides a late or retarded development, there is a precocity, where the transformation of the figure takes place too early. Both phenomena lead to problems which are discussed in the next chapter.

An assessment of the transformation of the figure entails some difficulty: a thin toddler looks older and may resemble a school-age child at first glance. However, if all the characteristic traits described above are carefully observed, there can be no confusion. A fat child seems like a toddler for longer, though the transformation of the limbs does take place and a practised observer will be able to tell a lot from a child's movements.

The loss of the milk teeth, which takes place when the child grows taller during the transitional stage, also deserves a mention. The milk teeth comprise the incisors, canines and the two molars behind the canines. Before the loss of the milk teeth the first permanent tooth emerges behind these two molars. Then the child loses the milk teeth, usually in the same order that they originally grew. In most cases the lower

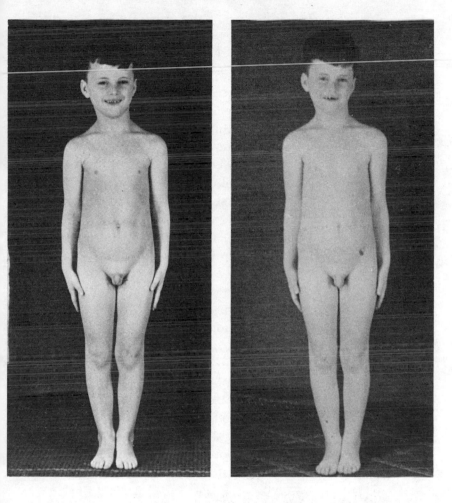

Figure 11. Age 6 years 8 months

Figure 12. Age 7 years 8 months.

incisors go first, followed by the upper incisors, and so on.

If this loss of milk teeth has not started before the first school year it is easy to find out whether the process is about to begin by seeing whether a molar has appeared behind the first two molars.

The loss of milk teeth, starting when a child is ready for school, continues throughout the entire second stage of seven years. Between the ages of ten and twelve another permanent molar appears behind the first and the child loses the first two molars. The canines go at the age of twelve, and by fourteen all the milk teeth have been replaced by permanent teeth.

Summarizing the whole of the third and fourth stages one could say that a child is physically ready for school when he has started to lose his milk teeth and has clearly reached the transitional stage.

The total transformation to the figure of the school-age child takes place during the first or possibly the second school year. Then, at the age of seven, the child's face changes significantly; a comparison of the child now with photographs of a year ago show how the last vestiges of the soft features of the small child have disappeared in a short while, how the chin, mouth and nose have grown, and how the expression in the eyes has become steadier.

2.5 Nine and ten-year-olds

During the following stage little seems to change either physiologically or psychologically until the beginning of puberty. However, we shall deal particularly with the important psychological crisis at the age of ten.

The ninth and tenth years of life form the period of *second growth in breadth*. The initially slender — often even thin — schoolchild now becomes more mature,

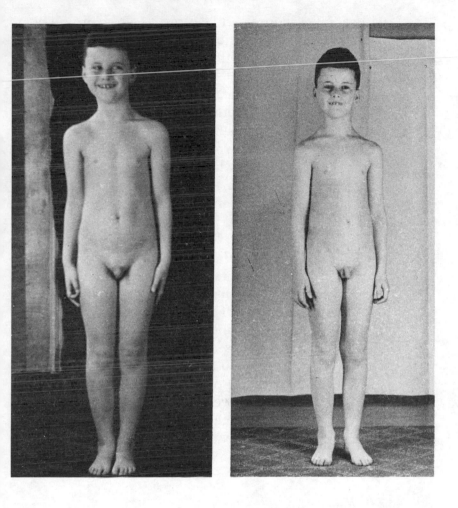

Figure 13. Age 8 years 8 months

Figure 14. Age 9 years 8 months.

with a fuller figure, and seems to grow in every direction at the same rate. However, careful observation reveals that the rate only appears to be the same.

During these years the trunk grows in height more, than in previous or in following years, and this marked growth is now accompanied by growth in breadth. Thus the musculature which had become visible just before the age of seven when the limbs were growing, disappears once again. The figure is no longer dominated by slim and energetic limbs, by the whole structure of movement in which the trunk was a flexible part of the body, but by the actual mass of the trunk. Some features of the toddler-figure are revealed once again. The thighs become powerful and broad with a layer of fat, quite different from the slim, muscular figure at the beginning of the period.

When a child is starting school he often has fresh, rosy- round cheeks and seems chubby, but when he is undressed this impression is different.

On the other hand, a fresh-faced, slim figure at nine or ten often proves to be well-padded when undressed, the muscles of the stomach and back in particular have become hidden to a greater extent than those of the limbs.

2.6 Pubescence

This period of second growth, which consists of more than simply 'filling out' all round, is followed by an even greater change which starts with the pubescent phase.

Actual puberty is preceded by growth in the limbs, just like that in the stage before the child reaches seven years of age. In this second spurt the child suddenly grows much taller and within a few months changes

40

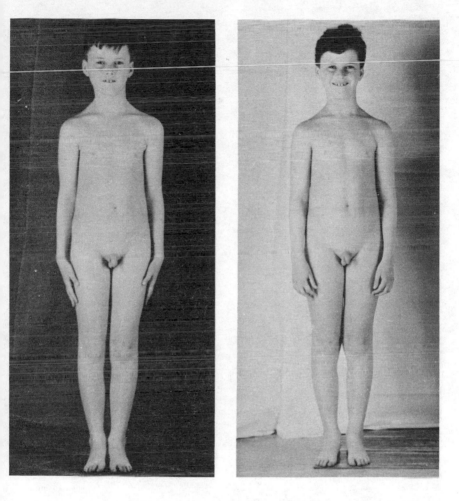

Figure 15. Age 10 years 9
months

Figure 16. Age 11 years 9
months.

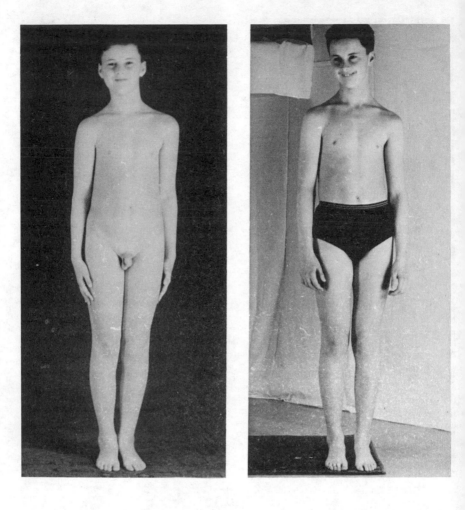

Figure 17. Age 12 years 9 months.

Figure 18. Age 14 years months.

from a stout child to a skinny beanpole. The process goes at such a rate that he will grow out of all his clothes in two or three months. The musculature becomes visible once again, and even though they may eat well children will become thinner during their twelfth year. Once again the limbs and their movement become a dominant feature.

The limbs grow in a singular way, becoming larger and less delicate at the extremities. Hands and feet grow fastest of all, followed by the lower arms and legs, while the upper arms and legs grow more slowly. As puberty approaches (fourteen years for boys, twelve for girls) there is therefore an imbalance in the figure as a whole; this is all the more noticeable as the proportions of the face also change during puberty.

As with the faster rate of growth of the ends of the limbs, the lower jaw also grows out and becomes more strongly defined, so that the face loses its rounded, childlike shape and acquires the exaggerated length of puberty. The nose also grows and for a while may look coarse and shapeless.

At the beginning of this stage (girls 10 to 11, boys 12 to 13), the second spurt of growth means that children are capable of greater physical achievements. They need to use their limbs intensively and outdo each other in running and swimming or wrestling, as though their lives depended on it. Children who exert themselves too much should be slowed down for the growth of the trunk has not caught up and the heart and lungs particularly are noticeably smaller in relation to the rest of the body during this period.

However, by the end of the pubescent phase and towards the beginning of puberty, the imbalance in the figure becomes such that the child's physical capacity is reduced. His figure may be gangling, his movements clumsy and insufficiently agile. He trips, steps on other people's toes, knocks over tables, especially when he doesn't feel comfortable.

The legs will now be relatively longest (often more than 60% of the total body length), while the trunk is short as well as thin.

2.7 Puberty

Actual puberty begins at this point of greatest imbalance. During the second stage of puberty the body achieves a new equilibrium, most clearly visible in the change of expression and the shape of the face. The disproportionate and rather coarse shape, with its long chin, large nose and still childlike eyes now becomes better proportioned as it grows broader, especially in the cheekbones, and as it acquires distinctly personal features. The expression is no longer so insecure and the adolescent looks at the outside world with an awareness of self; his will is revealed in a firmer mouth and chin. The whole face suggests that the adolescent wishes to form his own view of the world independently. This process is clearly shown in the illustrations of the growing boy (Figures 17 to 20).

The secondary sexual characteristics also start to develop now and the sexual glands start to function.

During this second stage of puberty the legs virtually stop growing and the trunk starts to grow longer. Almost all the growth that occurs now takes place in the trunk.

As a result the proportions of the body achieve an equilibrium that is immediately apparent - supported by a differentiation in the characteristic figures of the two sexes.

The process takes place in girls two or more years earlier than in boys. They develop more quickly so that the successive stages are shorter and often pass

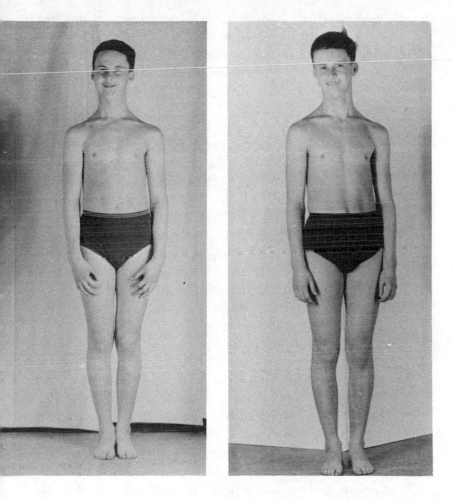

Figure 19. Age 15 years 8 months.

Figure 20. Age 16 years 8 months.

unnoticed. Pubescence, with the growth of the legs, often begins in girls towards the age of ten and continues through the eleventh and twelfth years. Actual puberty than starts at twelve or thirteen with the development of the breasts, rounded hips and growth of pubic hair.

In boys the phase starts at twelve or thirteen and continues well into the fourteenth year. The changes in the genitals, growth of pubic hair and breaking voice only become apparent at fourteen, and the last stage of physical puberty only takes place between fourteen and sixteen.

It could be argued that the slower development of boys adheres more strictly to a regular and rhythmic pattern of development, while this process is speeded up in girls and the rhythm is quickly disturbed. On the other hand, the last stage of maturation from young girl to womanhood takes longer.

Apart from the difference in development of boys and girls during puberty, the characteristics of the constitution that will develop also become clear. For example, in a tall, thin type the first stage of puberty will be most apparent and the figure which emerges during this stage will to some extent prevail throughout life. For a short, broad type this first stage is less apparent, while the second stage with the growth in the trunk lengthwise and in width is more clearly defined. These are only two extremes, as we are not concerned here with describing the constitution of different types in adulthood.

Towards the end of the first period of seven years constitutional factors have to be taken into account for a correct assessment of development, and should be considered to an even greater extent during puberty.

2.8 Maturation

Puberty is followed by a period of maturation when the figure develops into that of a youth or young girl. In boys the chest and shoulders are broader; in girls the hips and pelvic girdle grow out. The trunk is again a focal point in this third period of growth in breadth.

2.9 To full adulthood

Most writers describing child development stop at the end of this period of maturation, that is at eighteen years of age, but there is a further development to man or womanhood both psychologically and physically , which may affect their position in society or marriage. Men will grow a little taller, though the more sturdy build that also develops is more striking. The musculature, especially in the limbs, becomes more powerful and the whole frame also seems to grow heavier and stronger.

This description of the various stages of physical development is summarized in Table 1.

The two milestones in the physical development of the child are the emergence of the figure of a school age child, and puberty. Both are preceded by a period of growing taller.Thus development up to the age of twenty-one is divided into three main periods. During these attention is focused consecutively on the head, the trunk and the limbs. It is only during puberty that the transformation is so marked that the head, trunk and limbs all undergo considerable changes.

However, these changes in puberty can be summarized as the individualization and harmonization of the figure. Individualization affects first the sex of the child (the male or female figure develops), secondly, the constitution (the constitutional type of the individual now becomes

47

Age	
0 - 2 years	Baby form. *Head* predominates due to size and 'head start'.
2 - 5 years	Nursery-schoolchild. *Trunk* predominates. First growth in breadth.
5 - 7 years	Change to schoolchild. *Limbs* predominate. First growth in height.
7 - 8/9 years	Schoolchild form. *Face* becomes more individual.
9 - 12 (boys) 8 - 10 (girls)	Second growth in breadth. *Trunk* grows in length.
12 - 14 (boys) 10 - 12 (girls)	Pubescence. Second growth in length. *Limbs* grow.
14 - 16 (boys) 12 - 15 (girls)	Puberty. Individual *expression*. Firm gaze. Harmonizing of the *trunk*. Secondary sexual characteristics. Harmonization of the *limbs*.
16 - 18 (boys)	Maturing. Third growth in breadth. Boys develop shoulders, girls pelvis.
18 - 21 years	*Limb's* musculature and bones develop.

clearly recognizable), and thirdly, the personality now puts its mark on the whole figure; this is revealed particularly in the expression, facial features, bearing and carriage.

Harmonization here overcomes the one-sided tendency of growth before puberty, and changes the inharmonious figure to the final individual form.

If the specific aspects of the different shorter periods are studied more closely, it seems time and again that the periods when the individual emerges coincide with those when the head and face take precedence.

The periods when the trunk is dominant there is rest, with growth in breadth rather than in length. The periods when the limbs extend bring revolutionary changes and transitions to completely new stages of development.

Thus it is clear that the developmental rhythms are repeated in these three periods, each time at a higher level of individualization. To describe them we use the concept of metamorphosis as Goethe used it in his *Metamorphosis of Plants,* and we shall return to it again in Chapter 6 when discussing the soul.

3. The child up to the loss of the milk teeth

From a biological point of view, the first stage of the life of a child, when it is still completely protected by its parental home, can be divided into three: the period of infancy, the toddler stage, and the period of transition towards school age.

The new-born baby is quite helpless and totally dependent on his environment for everything. There is no sign of any soul life in the human sense, as he lies in the cradle making uncoordinated movements and sucking noises. He cries when he is cold and hungry, out of primitive instincts. When these primitive drives are satisfied, he is only capable of two activities, drinking and sleeping. The soul life of the child only gradually emerges during a development of many years, and this will be examined through the functions of thought, feeling and the will.

The infant is totally dependent on the environment. In other words, he completely entrusts himself to the environment with no reservations. When the warm, sweet milk flows into his body he experiences satisfaction not only with the tongue and the back of the mouth; the whole body, including the little kicking feet and tiny grasping hands, is involved in tasting. Tasting is done with the whole being; the soul opens out completely for the outside world with an all-pervading sense of delight. When the baby has drunk his fill, and falls back replete, he sinks into a satisfied state of unconsciousness until the feeling of hunger again conjures up a reaction of dissatisfaction, and once again the baby expresses his dissatisfied feeling with his whole body. He screams and kicks, waving his arms and throwing his body around, until it is covered in sweat and completely exhausted. When he is breast fed again after being changed, he will first greedily suck the milk and gradually become calmer. A quiet glow spreads over the whole body, and after a little while he can let go for a moment, looking round with great satisfaction, only to seek the source of the sweet milk once again, and continue to drink.

Thus the first weeks of life pass with drinking and sleeping, and drinking and sleeping. When the baby is awake the eyes often wander through space independently, so that he may look alarmingly cross-eyed; he is not yet able to move eyes, arms and legs purposefully. After a few weeks it may happen that when the mother looks over the cradle the baby looks at her for a moment and a small smile comes to his lips. This is a moment of a great joy for the mother. For the first time some aspect of the new person has shone out through his eyes; he has laughed for the first time. Now the mother knows that it is a human child lying in the cradle, for an animal cannot laugh, and although this is not conscious recognition, she has had her first meeting with her child. Thus the failure of a baby to laugh is always a sign of a child who is not developing normally, or that development is retarded or deviant.

After this, such 'meetings' occur more and more often, and the parents can be certain that the child's consciousness is developing. This awakening during the first months of life is coupled with another phenomenon: initially the child only really woke up to take more food, and then would fall asleep again. Short periods of waking alternated with much longer periods of deep sleep. When the child becomes more

52

conscious, the time spent sleeping decreases and the time spent awake increases, as is clearly shown in the diagrams below.

Ratio of waking to sleeping in a 24-hour period.

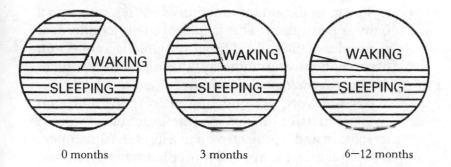

| 0 months | 3 months | 6–12 months |

Few people realize what enormous physical feats are achieved during the first months of life: in the first five months the child actually doubles his birth weight. Just imagine what adults would have to do in order to double their weight in five months. It would involve a fattening process in which one couldn't take a step or think of anything but could only eat and sleep. It would involve tremendous concentration at a physical level, comparable only to the training of a world championship sprinter.

However, this is exactly what happens to a newborn baby. All the not yet apparent faculties are concentrated on a single goal, growing; everything else is subordinated to this.

Such an enormous physical feat is achieved only once in a person's life. The next times in which a baby doubles his weight lasts much longer: up to the age of two, then again to the age of eight, and lastly to the age of sixteen. Thus there is a strong decrease in the intensity of the growth rate after the first months of life.

The second and subsequent periods of doubling in weight are achieved in very different circumstances. The child's waking hours have increased. His functions are no longer exclusively aimed at a physical level; all sorts of activities have developed which belong to conscious life.

The most important function of consciousness in a baby is perception. This is part of the unconditional surrender of the child. The whole child is a collection of perceptions, one might say, an entire sensory organ. All his psychological activity is aimed at finding out about the world around him. Perception is by no means a passive process in which the outside world streams in and is projected on to a light sensitive plate, a popular image borrowed from photography. In fact, the activity is centred in interest in the outside world. Something must be activated from the inside to meet the impressions coming in from the outside, if such impressions are to be perceived. A retarded child receives just as many impressions from outside as a normal child, but the retarded child is unable to perceive them, because he lacks the inner active interest for the outside world that is present in normal children. In a small child this active interest is still part of his desires, and not part of his conscious will, as it may be at a later age. However, desire is the precursor of the will, or in other words, the will is desire directed by the self.

Thus it may be said that a small child is a sensory organ in which desire (the will) is active.

The surrender to the world takes place with a force which at a later age can only be compared with the complete surrender of a religious person. The element directed to the divine being in religion is active at a physical level in the child. Thus Rudolf Steiner, in his lectures on education, described it as a 'religious

54

surrender to the environment' and called it a 'physical religion'.

This active surrender means that a small child is a creature of imitation. Everything that is learned in the first stage of life is learned by imitation. This is carried out with varying degrees of intensity, depending on the child's character, type and temperament, but in principle the child's spiritual life develops in this way during the first period.

Imitation is much further-reaching than merely the echoing of speech in the environment or a playful copying of activities. Even before the child is able to do this, it assimilates a great deal from its environment, and paradoxically one can conclude that the less consciously a child perceives what is around him, the more such perceptions penetrate his soul. Before a child is able to be conscious of his perceptions and assimilate them to make them his own, impressions are deepest and may penetrate the most profound unconscious levels of the soul. They remain there, forming a foundation for later more conscious experiences.

Undoubtedly psychoanalysis, despite its one-sided tendency, has the great merit of opening our eyes to the relation between the subconscious and the first experiences of childhood.

During this first period of development parents have a great responsibility towards their child. For it is precisely those things that are not consciously experienced that later on will influence particular moods, feelings or behaviour.

The child whose soul is completely open to the world not only perceives his father's actions when he turns away in irritation and walks out at the door, but will also assimilate the moral contents of such gestures; these remain in the depths of his subconscious. Whether a person goes through life with an unwavering trust in the goodness of the world as the foundation of his spiritual life, despite any number of trials and tribulations, or whether he goes through life filled with suspicion and lacking in joy, even though everything has gone his way, these things can be greatly influenced by the environment created by his parents during the first years of his life.

From a developmental point of view, people influence children during the first years of life by what they *are*, by expressing the trust they have acquired, and morality in their actions.

For a baby it is quite meaningless when an adult coos sweet nothings in a silly childish voice, and then turns away to talk about other more important things. Anyone who is with the child should really be with it with total interest and great warmth, complete respect and a moral will to help this little human being on its way through life. During this period the infant, who apparently understands nothing, intensely assimilates the deeper spiritual content surrounding it.

3.1 The transition from infancy to the toddler stage

The child's inner activity which was apparent in his interest in the outside world, also helps him to discover his own body. If this process is carefully observed, one can see how the child's own body is also an unknown part of the outside world. Hands, waving through the field of vision, are discovered and used as the first toy. Then the legs are discovered and grasped, only to disappear suddenly, nowhere to be found. This is the same comic performance as that of a young kitten trying to catch its own tail. Once the baby has discovered his own body in that part of the world which is his, he can gradually use it to discover other parts of the world.

The child laboriously rising from the horizontal position, must find a new orientation. It is worth thinking about this process of becoming erect, for after the first laughter, it is one of the most characteristic expressions of the child.

All the higher mammals live their entire lives on the horizontal plane and do not assume a vertical position, not even the kangaroo or the gorilla, as is clearly demonstrated by their skeletons. In humans a vertical stance is related to a differentiation in the function of arms and legs. Only the legs are used for locomotion; the arms are freed from this task, and can now be used as a tool. They become organs of expression and perform higher tasks. In animals all four limbs are used for locomotion, even in monkeys with four hands. In human beings the differentiation between arms and legs is so far-reaching that in a child's physical development the arms follow the growth rhythm of the trunk, and not that of the legs.

The process of rising normally begins during the second half of the first year, when the child sits up, crawls, and pulls himself up, and it is completed during the second year when he learns to walk. It is only when the child is walking steadily that he loses his baby figure with the folds in the thighs and little cushions on the arms and hands.

Thus we think of this stage when a baby learns to walk as the end of babyhood and of learning to talk as the beginning of the period of transition towards the toddler. In certain cases these periods may partly overlap.

During the first stage of assuming a vertical position the arms are still used for locomotion when the baby crawls or pulls himself up. They are only freed when he takes his first step.

A great deal can be learned about the potential of

the child from the way in which he goes through this process of assuming a vertical position. This characteristic activity is one of the first to indicate his biographical potential. For example, there is the child who has been able to sit for a long time and who is quite capable of standing up, but will only slowly pull himself up on the bars of the play-pen to step around, holding on to the edge, not crossing over to an opposite corner for months, but then immediately taking hold of the edge again. Such a child will prefer to sit down and crawl as soon as it has no help. Another child will work himself up from a sitting position in the middle of the room, wobbling backwards and forwards, waving his arms through the air and falling over, to repeat the same thing dozens of times, until finally he stands, swaying to and fro like a tree in a storm. Then again he will stand in the middle of the room, all alone, lift up a foot and topple over, repeating this many times until he has taken his first step. The first words this child will speak are: 'No! *Me* do it!' When you follow the development of these two different types of children, you will see that the stage of standing up and walking was characteristic of its later life.

Once the child is walking, babyhood is over. During this period the perceptive process has awakened, and the child has conquered part of the outside world.

The first type of memory awakens (see the Chapter 8 for the three types of memory); as a result of rhythmic repetition certain reflexes and habits are formed. However, the process of thought, the conscious processing and combination of perceptions has not yet become apparent. This will only develop once the child starts to speak during the next stage.

3.2 Transition to the toddler stage: Walking, talking, thinking

While the child was learning to assume an upright position, another purely human capacity was also developing, that is, speech.

Previously he made all sorts of noises: crying when he was discontented, gurgling and babbling to express feelings of contentment and joy.

Initially a child is orientated towards the *ah* sound, the vowel in which a stream of air passes out unhindered and which expresses the whole direction of the inner activity in wonder at the opening of the outside world.

'Dada', 'papa, and 'mama' are the first intelligible sounds. The first words are accompanied only by certain feelings, rather than by particular images or representations. A greater variety of sounds only develops as the baby continues to move about in an upright position, so that his arms are no longer necessary for locomotion. He only begins to speak whole words when he has started to learn to walk.

Learning to speak is a very complicated process, both physiologically and psychologically. Psychologically the centre of speech in the brain is formed at this stage along with the centre for the hand, which instinctively grasps the world (in right-handed children with the right hand, in left-handed children with the left hand). We see how with the acquisition of speech a foundation is laid for conscious soul life which is determined by two sources. One is given by the physical body, from which needs and drives penetrate, evoking feelings and impulses to act. All the feelings of pleasure and displeasure and the related activities during the first year, such as eating and moving, are based on this physical source. The other is the spiritual potential, which forms the focal point of the self in the adult. The activities derived from this also penetrate soul life and are often in opposition to the physical drives. These are the forces related to our morality, making us into moral beings.

When children learn to speak, a spiritual order is laid down. However, it is not yet such that it emanates from the individual self. It could be called a collective human spiritual order.

Language reflects the spiritual values which are dominant in man at any given moment. It comes to the child from the human environment, and the child assimilates it by imitation. Before the individual self becomes active, he takes in something of the collective self from the environment. For the time being this acts as a guideline in the life of the child, forming the first counterweight to a complete supremacy of physical drives.

Language is the collective spiritual heritage of a group of people who feel more closely related by this than by anything else. However, language was not 'thought up' by people. It contains values which are far beyond the individual and collective knowledge of the those who speak it. The concepts 'spirit of language' and 'folk spirit' no longer have a specific content in our time; they are considered as the sum of a number of characteristics of a particular language and people. However, language is not only part of the human spiritual world, but also of the spiritual cosmos.

The vowels and consonants contain creative principles: for instance the diastole in the *ah*, is an opening to the outside world, while the systole in the *oo* expresses a withdrawal from the outside world. Vowels and consonants are an aspect of formative forces which operate in cosmic creation. Together they form the Logos, the Word, which, according to St John, was 'in the beginning'. In modern terminology they might be called 'models', systematized information.

The language of a particular people, with its characteristic vowels and consonants, is used to creatively name and speak of the world. The fact that other peoples use different names for the same object simply means that they experience things differently because of their outlooks. To learn a particular language as one's mother tongue influences experience of the outside world in a particular way.

The child experiences his language not only as a tool to communicate certain experiences as quickly and easily as possible, but also a finely differentiated spiritual structure. In other words, language is not merely a facility enabling a form of spiritual exchange, but is actually itself a structural element of the spirit. This is why the mother tongue is so important in forming the structure of the personality - we are so inextricably bound up with it that we experience it as a part of our own essence, and we can enjoy its beauty and love it as a much-loved friend, and feel threatened to the very core when we are in danger of losing it. This is not surprising, for language itself helps to create us.

When the child learns to speak, he comes into contact with this complicated world. When he no longer needs his hands for locomotion, and the hands are therefore free for the higher functions of life, the speech centre develops in the brain next to the centre for the hands.

The child endlessly copies what he hears, and the treasure of language, as well as the ability to speak are acquired with an incomparable energy. Just as he achieved the remarkable physical feat of doubling his weight during the first five months of life, there is an equally wonderful spiritual achievement during the second and third years of life.

A great deal can be learned from the child's character during this period, just as when he learned to walk.

In the first place, children enter the world of language with varying degrees of enthusiasm. In addition, there are children who merely assimilate the language around them, imitating passively and rather slavishly, while others decisively create their own means of expression. These children will call objects and people by the usual imitated name, as well as by a name they have coined themselves. In this way we see how children still have a creative ability now surviving only in great poets, and are able to create a word to express their personal experience from the essence of sound. Other children speak indistinctly for a long time, unable to assimilate language; such children often turn out to have a stronger visual capacity at a later stage, though sometimes it is a sign of a general backwardness.

The first thing a child learns to do is to name objects in the outside world: table, chair, baby, cow, tree; the child recognizes the object and names it. However, this apparently simple task is a symptom of a completely new attitude to the world; it is the first step in setting oneself against the outside world, for up to now the small child has experienced it as being entirely linked to himself. Thus learning to speak brings a breaking of the ties between the core of the self and the surrounding world, a process that only ends with puberty.

When speaking goes beyond the mere naming of objects, and the child starts to put words together to form sentences, thought processes begin which then develop in concepts related to speech.

Thus the first concepts have a concrete content, though they are concerned with totalities. There was a time only a few decades ago when it was thought that children developed the concept of a tree by seeing the object consisting of trunk, branches and leaves, and then another object consisting of the same parts, though with a different shape, so that it would understand that the sum of the parts (trunk, branches and leaves) was a tree. It was thought that concepts were built up from elements. We now know that this view is incorrect. It was found that the child first has a concept of the totality and only much later distinguishes the constituent elements.

A child understands the concept of a tree as such, and will call a tree which it has never seen before, and which is a completely different shape from all the other trees it has seen, by the same name. The first concepts are vague and not strictly defined, though they are rich and comprehensive, and full of mysterious depth. These rich, childish concepts later turn into the sharply defined dry concepts of adults, which have gradually lost their experiential content; in contrast, the concept of the child still has life and colour.

Plato had yet another idea of conceptual development: he saw the learning of the concept of a tree as a memory of the divine idea of a tree. It is a memory because the spiritual part of man is itself derived from a world of divine ideas; on earth it meets the material reflection of these ideas, and recognizes them, so that the concept of a tree can be understood. Socrates declared that the best thinker was the man with the best memory.

Two thousand years later, this view of the creation of concepts in human beings fits in with recent research regarding the total character of the concepts of children.

Thinking develops with and through speech. Thus the first concepts are concretely related to the outside world, where the first 'object concepts' are learned, such as table, tree, cat, and so on.

During the next stage a verb is added to the name of the object: fire burns, pussy jumps, sister cries. The outside world is not only interpreted as *being*, but is understood as *active*.

With the first function the child conquers the world of space; with the second, the world of time, for actions take place in time. This is why the concept of time only starts to dawn in the child during the second stage. He starts to differentiate between yesterday and tomorrow. In addition he also starts to understand various connections, first simple and later more complicated, which are related to various actions. For example, a two-year-old child playing in a room, who manages to open a door and walk into a corridor, has to be kept in the room. It is enough to turn the key, and the child will walk to the door, fiddle with the lock, pulling the key, and is unable to open the door. When the child has reached the second half of the third year of life, he suddenly sees the connection: he fiddles with the lock, pulls on the key and manages to open the door. Now the key must be taken out of the lock if the child is to be kept in the room. Such small developments are symptoms of developing associations. In normal children they follow in such rapid succession that one is not aware of them. In retarded children, they are milestones in development. The normal child will develop a consciousness of self in his third year, and a separate chapter is devoted to this later on.

The child's environment at the time of learning to speak is of great importance for the development of character. During the first year of life it was the spirit of morality which had the greatest influence on the child, but now it is the way language is spoken around the child. The spiritual structure of the developing child depends to a large extent on whether the mother tongue is spoken well or badly during this time. The child will be able to form a close relationship with the language in the deepest core of his self, if the mother tongue is spoken clearly, without slurring or dropping consonants and vowels, and with a grammar reflecting a structure and expressing the subtleties of language by a varied use of words and phrases. In this way the child is rooted in the spiritual structures common to a people, and saved from greedily grasping later at artificial national passions.

It is not for nothing that a child is born in a particular country. The self has the possibility of developing in a certain way in the spiritual ambience of that country. If this starting point is on firm ground it will help him to understand other peoples, as he is anchored in the culture of his own people, and in this way achieves a truly free interchange.

Additionally, the greater or lesser differentiation of the language in the environment influences the differentiation of the child's thinking. This holds good both for the image itself, which develops as objects are named, and for logical thought processes, which develop together with syntactical processes. As regards the former, a precise choice of words in which small differences are sharply distinguished also produces precise images. As regards the latter, a proper syntax forms the basis for the dynamics of thinking.

It is self-evident that a language with a greater vocabulary allows for a greater differentiation of imagery. The syntax of different languages also produces different ways of thinking, as is clearly illustrated by comparing Latin and Germanic languages. However, even within a single linguistic family there may be important differences. For example, in German it is possible to encapsulate an image in a single word by joining words together, while the same image in English requires a phrase. In the first case the concept can be more speedily identified, while in the second case, the description allows for greater flexibility.

All this may seem unimportant, but in reality it has a great influence on the structure of personality. Thus learning to speak different languages means more than a mere ease of communication or aesthetic enjoyment; it represents an unequalled enrichment of our whole inner life and a further differentiation and refinement in our thought.

The mother tongue, which is used in daily life, has the greatest influence, and it is important that it is presented to the imitating child in all its richness, and in all its inner structural complexity.

The experience of teaching deaf children proves the importance of acquiring language for thinking. It has been shown that if children do not learn to master language at the 'sensitive stage', they can gain 'object concepts' at a later stage, but they will have more difficulty with abstract concepts and advanced thinking.

If the children are taught at an early age to master syntax as well as vocabulary, the results are much better and the shortcomings of their thought processes are much reduced. The following case may serve as an example.

Wendy, an eighteen-year-old deaf girl, was working in a sewing room of a Dutch institution. She had been sent to a school for the deaf at quite a late age, where she had learned to read, write, lip-read and speak, and had been trained as a seamstress. One day an exciting event took place in the house; the flag was raised, the children wore sashes and orange ribbons in their hair, and although it was a working day, there was no work.

Wendy asked in her toneless voice: 'Why party?' On being told that it was the Queen's birthday, she asked, 'What is Queen?'

We all tried to explain the concept of 'queen' to Wendy in various different ways. 'Head of state.' 'Don't understand.' 'Lady on throne.' 'Don't understand...' We had to give up, and Wendy simply accepted that it was a holiday.

By contrast, we remember how a three-year-old can be told stories: 'Once upon a time there was a queen who wanted to have a princess ...' 'Queen' and 'princess' are concepts which are initially rather vague with a totality of splendour and size, but which gradually and unnoticed, become more profound, and after a few years they have become rich contents of the child's soul. Assimilating this content in an abstract way is only partially successful.

This concludes the period of learning to walk, speak and think. We saw how the child orientated himself in space as an upright being, motivated by an inner need for movement, and then how he mastered his mother tongue through imitation, in this way creating the possibility of developing thought as the first conscious psychological function from the still undifferentiated understanding of life. Thus the beginning of the development of thought occurs between the second and the third years of life. At this stage, thinking is still mainly realistic, as it is concerned with establishing order in the world of perception. The fact that it changes in nature during later periods of development is clear from the following chapters.

3.3 Emotional life before the change of teeth

The emotional life of the infant swings back and forth between feelings of content and discontent. Of course, these are always a feature of emotional life, but in the infant they are completely dependent on the vital functions of the physical organism; they rise into the soul from below.

During the period of transition to the toddler stage, when the child is learning to walk, talk and think, the outside world is increasingly involved in the development of feelings. A small child is happy and gay when he feels healthy, and when the outside world creates pleasant situations; miserable and tearful when his health is poor, or the outside world crosses him.

Emotions, even in adults, are marked by a lesser degree of consciousness than is thinking. Our feelings are at the level of a semi-conscious dream state. Therefore in investigating the emotional life of the child, we have to look for the moment when feelings acquire that semi-conscious, dreamlike quality for the first time. For this it is necessary that feelings are not only a reaction to physical events or the immediate outside world, but that there may also be other influences.

Thus the awakening consciousness of self in about the third year of life is a condition for the awakening of the semi- conscious emotion. The child realizes that he can say 'no' to the world, and by saying 'no' his own self is felt as being stronger. This is the beginning of the period of obstinacy, the first negative stage.

When the experience of the self is present even without going against the outside world, this negative phase comes to an end. It is only then that the emotions can develop from an interaction of

68

influences from above and below. The best way to study this is by observing the character of the child's play.

Children begin to play at a very early age. They may even be said to play during the first few months of life. They discover that the hands moving through their field of vision can be guided, and these become their first toys. Then they find their feet, and these are even more fun, for they are constantly lost and can then be refound. This is followed by a teething ring or rattle, then building bricks and boxes which can be endlessly placed on top of each other or next to each other.

However, there is one thing that all the games during the first years of life have in common: the child plays with those things that happen to be within his horizon. If a doting aunt gives a child an unsuitable toy, it's enough to simply put it away in the cupboard. After a few tears the child will go on to play with something else. However, if he comes across the toy again when mother is cleaning up, he will want to have it again. This characteristic that small children play with anything that is available *now*, leads to problems in a family of children of different ages.

If older children are playing with dolls, the toddler will toddle up and want to play with the dolls as well. The mother may say. 'Ellie is so small. Let Ellie play with the dolls, and you go and build.' The older ones may have started to build after some protest, but then the doll is thrown aside. Once again, Ellie wants to join in, and in her enthusiasm she will throw over the towers and destroy houses and garages. This could go on for ever, if the older ones don't escape to play outside.

This example shows how the child's play is still connected with the environment. In imagination he is able to stand back, to name and understand objects, but his feelings are still entirely caught up in the world, locked in the 'here and now', and only able to respond to the world with joy or sorrow. This is why joy and sadness can alternate so quickly: 'now he laughs, now he cries'.

Although this reaction may be considered as a pendulum of the emotions, it cannot really be considered as individual 'feeling' in the real sense of the word. Reacting to the outside world emotionally only becomes feeling in a real sense when a structured inner life has developed, which experiences through feeling. Animals also react to the outside world with content and discontent. However, an animal does not reach a similar life of feeling, but remains tied to its environment.

In a child one must find the moment when he withdraws for the first time from exclusively experiencing the environment and reveals a structured emotional world: that moment can be identified as the birth of feeling, just as the birth of thinking is described as the moment at which separate perceptions and images are associated to form a complete interrelation.

In about the fourth year of life a great change takes place in the play of small children. Until then they were entirely concerned with anything round about. Now the child takes a step back from this arbitrary environment. As previously feelings were connected to the perception of the vital functions and of the outside world, now a new force begins to develop in the emotional life. The child sees himself as separate from the outside world. This force can best be described as 'creative imagination' which stands in contrast to the outside world, changing it according to inner needs.

Play activity becomes much more intense. It is

fascinating to come into a room and find a child playing. The carpet has become a whole new world; the central pattern is the sea, the lines around it are roads, and under the table there is a house. You cannot walk into the centre or you'll get wet feet. Bricks and cushions are trains, cars and mountains; a complete house is built under the table, with a living room, bedroom and kitchen. You realize that the child is not merely *playing* that there is a house under the table - the space actually is a house. The child has linked his imagination with reality, which is now seen through the imagination. A world of play and fairy-tales is produced by the child himself, in which everything is possible if the imagination wishes it to be. The time has come for seeing the world with charmed eyes, when colours and relations can change as he wishes.

A lady once told me how, when she was eighteen she revisited the house where she had lived as a small child. Expectantly she went into the garden to rediscover the old world, but she was very disappointed. She merely saw an ordinary garden with bushes, and a small ditch. She asked: 'But mother, what happened to the wood that used to be there on the left?' And her mother answered: 'There was never a wood. Everything is just as it was.' 'But I'm sure there used to be a wood there. We used to walk by it with our dolls' prams. It was a large dark wood. I can see it before me.' The wood had existed only in the imagination of the playing child, where it was more real than a real wood could ever have been.

The time has now come for the child to play without restraints. Any object, such as a matchbox or a piece of coloured glass is infinitely valuable, and the child looks for ways to act out his imagination on his own and with others.

Adults should take this play seriously and enrich the inner life by providing new content as well as external possibilities. If there is no time or too little space to do this in a busy household, this is the time to take the child to a nursery school, where fairy-tales are told. These are as necessary for the child as his bread and butter; he needs the space to act out his imagination. A pile of bricks, some boards and a few sturdy old tables, some empty boxes, paper, water-colours, crayons and sticky paper are essential in the nursery school. Finally there should be a chest of pieces of material which the child can use to dress up, and the teacher must be warm and young at heart. All this makes up the ideal play school.

Often the problem with play groups is that there are a number of three-year-olds who have not yet reached the stage of creative imagination, and are therefore unable to enter into the spirit of the thing. It is best to take these children on one side, or keep them at home, until they are ready, but unfortunately circumstances often do not allow for this, and there is nothing we can do about it. One teacher can easily cope with a large group who are really ready for play school, as they merely need the occasional helping hand to continue their imaginative play. In addition, her task consists of an intuitive understanding of when a game should be brought to an end before it ends in tears, because children do not know when to stop, and often overestimate their own physical capacity.

There is another noteworthy aspect of this period of creative imagination: the sudden transition from the world of the imagination to the real world, and vice-versa. The same chairs which had been used minutes before as a train, or a table which was a house, suddenly turn into ordinary chairs to sit on and tables to eat at when it's time for dinner, and immediately after dinner they turn back into a train and a house, if this is allowed. We met this characteristic of feeling before when we said: 'Now he laughs, now he cries'. Above we were concerned with the polarity between delight and sadness; this time it is the polarity between the imagination and reality.

Fairy-tales also originated in this creative imagination during a stage when men still lived within such forces. The fairy-tales which are true folk tales are always concerned with great truths of life and death, good and evil, the growth of the soul in humility, and its strengthening in chivalry. The *content* is formed by profound truths, coming from the world of the still semi-conscious creative spirit, the *form* is that of the childish creative fantasy. This is why it is meaningless to talk of 'lies' in fairy-tales. Wolves cannot speak, so it is a lie to tell children they can; Grannie and Little Red Riding Hood are eaten up by the wolf - what a gruesome, frightening story, and anyway it is another lie to say that it would be possible for them still to be alive when they are cut out of the wolf's stomach. I have a story book about Little Red Riding Hood which dates from the beginning of the century. Little Red Riding Hood was not led astray by the wolf, she wasn't eaten up and the wolf didn't die. But what remains of the fairy-tale? It is a horribly trite, moralizing story which wouldn't interest any child. The slumbering soul of the child has an intuitive knowledge of the secrets of life and death, of being imprisoned in the bonds of the dark earth, and of resurrection from that darkness. In his own body, unconsciously, but realistically, the child experiences the life forces causing it to grow, and, as consciousness awakes, the death forces countering the life forces. Fairy-tales form a link with these great eternal questions, so that his spirit can awaken and feel at

73

home on the earth. The form of the fairy-tale corresponds exactly with the structure of his own soul. Even if you only count what children learn of facts and human relationships, and how, listening with enjoyment, they are able to assimilate many complicated concepts, telling fairy-tales must be rated a pleasant and useful educational activity.

Thus in the fifth year of life the child is at a peak of indefatigable creative play. When you observe a child of this age in the sand-pit, you will see how the play is exclusively concerned with *activities* in an endless flow of creative forces. In a later chapter we shall discuss where such forces come from, but now merely notice the way in which they are revealed. In the sand-pit the child bakes sand-cakes, pressing thirty, forty or even fifty cakes on a board with a few small moulds. What does he do when the board is full up? Does he stop, full of pride, when the work is finished? No, the board is full, and for a minute the game is interrupted. One child will call out: 'What a lot of sand-cakes we've got, Mum.' But the game must go on, and energetically the board is turned over and filled up again. Sometimes you have to join in and taste a sand-cake, but the production line is barely interrupted. The child is essentially concerned not with the final product, but with the *joy of creation*. When he has finished, he will forget all about his cakes. You can see how such toddlers will make a mountain with a tunnel through it. When it is finished one of them will jump on it while the others cheer. Then they'll make another one.

Little girls endlessly make and remake their dollies' beds. Toddlers enthusiastically begin new colouring books, scribbling and drawing page after page, immediately turning over another page and starting a new drawing. Sometimes they even draw more or less the same thing on every page. They do not look back once a drawing is finished, for they are concerned with the creative process itself, with making something.

You can hear how children endlessly repeat the same nursery rhyme or poem, over and over again. A healthy toddler doesn't know when to stop, and when he does, it's either to begin a new game, or because, in the end, he is tired or hungry and his natural reaction is to take a break.

The toddler is preoccupied with rhythm during the creative period. Songs accompany certain repeated activities in a particular rhythm. The repetition of the creative process in a seemingly endless rhythm is typical of play during this period. The child can remember things in a rhythmical form for which it has no abstract memory. This is the secret of traditional nursery rhymes. He will listen to the same story every evening, again and again, and will even enjoy it more as it is told more often.

A four-and-a-half-year-old boy was told the story of the Three Kings at Christmas and this made a great impression on him. It was told again and again every evening right through until the end of August, and he still wanted to hear only about the Three Kings. His parents found it very difficult to remain enthusiastic throughout the summer about the three wise men from the east, but the child would listen wide- eyed, not allowing any attempt at shortening the story or leaving out a single detail. In the course of the months the story had been extended with descriptions and events which do not appear in any official version of the story of the Three Kings, but once they had been incorporated, there was no leaving them out.

This is also the secret of the seemingly inexhaustible play of children. As long as it is carried out rhythmically, it is not tiring, for it relates to the

75

rhythmic processes, such as respiration and circulation, which never tire either. It is what is unrhythmical and intellectual in play that tires the children.

This form of play - play for its own sake - only changes at about the age of six. Gradually, almost unnoticed, the child's play changes slightly, and at a particular moment, usually around the sixth birthday, coinciding roughly with the loss of the first milk teeth, it becomes clear that the child is entering a new stage of life.

3.4 *The development of the will*

During the first years of the child's life, there is not really any conscious will. The first expressions of activity are based in the organism's vital functions. During the subsequent toddler period, drives direct behaviour, such as wanting to go outside or stay in, wanting a particular toy. At this time a mother may say that her child is 'strong-willed', but in fact this is not really a will, but a drive. The will is the force which can direct drives or is able to set goals beyond the immediate gratification of drives. The will starts to develop during the period of active imagination when behaviour is based on creative play, which itself is impelled by waves of feeling in rhythmic repetition.

This was play for its own sake, not aimed at achieving a goal that the child had set. At about the age of six this changes for the first time, and now play does have a goal. The child no longer follows only the forces of his creative imagination, but sets himself a *goal* which he wants to achieve. A heap of sand with a tunnel through it must be so made that a car or train can be pushed through, and an adjoining bridge must be able to bear weight. The younger brother or sister who suddenly jumps on top of this creation should watch out, for although this would have been cheered six months earlier, it now gives rise to heated quarrels because: 'It was so good and I wanted to go on building it tomorrow!'

For the first time something in the child has awakened which can be said to be part of his true will. He stands in the world now with a conscious will, he has a goal he wants to achieve, Up to this time his behaviour was based first on drives and later on the productive stream of imaginative play; now it rises above this level and represents the first appearance of the will. It is only when the child has reached this point and sets himself goals that he is ready for school, for only now is the structure of the soul such that he can start to learn.

However, at the same time that the conscious will awakens, the child's whole attitude to the outside world changes. When he played, unconcerned with results and merely for the joy of creation, he did not experience the objective value of his achievement in any sense. When he needed a boat to sail on the sea of the carpet, any building brick, piece of card or box would do. The magic spectacles of fantasy immediately saw the necessary ship. Thus the actual object at most represents a crystallization of the imagination. A child can find an unsightly piece of rag and enthusiastically show what a beautiful bag it is for his doll. An adult will gladly agree that it is beautiful, even with no idea how to hold it for it to look like a bag. All this is different when the change is taking place in the child, indicating that he is ready for school. Now he wishes the paper boat he has made to look like a real boat and wants it really to float. He gradually acquires an awareness of his own inability to achieve in reality those things he sees in his imagination. He asks for help from adults whenever he lacks the capacity for designing and creating the things he wants to make.

77

The force of respect develops in the child's soul with the realization of things he cannot do, and the expectation that adults can. For this respect to develop, the child must see his world hierarchically, and must think of himself as being at a different level from adults and endowed with different capacities from theirs.

Toddlers certainly do not have such respect. For them the whole world within their horizon belongs to them. The self and the outside world are one. Father and mother, home and garden belong to him as much as do his hands and feet. The older toddler sees himself consciously as separate from the outside world, though the feelings which stream out from him are so powerful that he still does not experience it in separation. After all, he is constantly discovering his own essence out there by means of his active imagination. It is only when the child experiences his own inability to act creatively in that outside world that there is a real division between that and the self. The child is now lonely and helpless, and it is only the fact that his emotions are still anchored in the creative imagination that forestalls a crisis such as that of puberty. Nevertheless, this period could really be called a first puberty.

The respect of the child for the adult soon becomes boundless. Just as he does everything with his whole being, so he now respects with his whole being. This respect usually crystallizes around a particular person, and the choice is often surprising. Social position, wealth and status are absolutely irrelevant. The person who is respected has a certain *ability*. He or she must be able to fold a paper boat, mend a broken doll, repair a toy car; must be able to answer all the child's questions about plants and animals, angels and cars, gnomes and stars. The family in which father or mother is the respected person is lucky indeed, but often it is someone else: the greengrocer, an uncle, a neighbour, a teacher at school - any of these may be chosen. The child's judgment is quite different from ours.

Thus a girl of almost six surprised her father who had mended the family's shoes during the war and was now making a courageous attempt to sew a button on to his trousers. After watching silently for a long time, she said: 'Daddies are much cleverer than mummies because daddies can sew too, and mummies can't mend shoes.'

At this stage the child judges people by what they *can do*, not by what they *know*.

Once this respect is kindled a new educational principle takes the place of imitation: the child becomes receptive to authority. Authority and respect are to each other what the key is to the lock. Authority without respect is slavery. Authority can only be an educational principle when it is inwardly accepted through respect.

A child who is ready for school profoundly desires to feel respect for the outside world, and this is why he can be led at school by authority.

This awakening of respect and the accompanying receptivity for authority is easy to observe in behaviour. Unless he is shy, a four or five-year-old child, absorbed in play as he enters a room where his father is talking to a friend about important matters will quite disregard the adults' conversation. Daddy has to join in the game or the child pulls at his trouser leg because Daddy has to fix a wheel which has come off a car. 'Daddy, listen, you've got to make the wheel,' or 'You have to come and play.' If the father then answers: 'No, Johnny. You shouldn't interrupt grown-ups when they're talking to each other,' this

79

leads to disappointment or sadness, as Johnny is not yet able to understand such a demand, and it is natural for the whole outside world to enter his imagination, as this is the only world he knows. It is only when he begins to distinguish between the two worlds, his own and that of the adults, that it gradually becomes possible for him to understand such a reply and to accept it. However, it takes a few years for him to reach this new stage.

In Chapter 1 we discussed in some detail the physical changes which take place when the child is ready for school. Experience has confirmed the view that psychological and physical maturity go together. The growth of the limbs and the development of a slimmer, more agile figure coincide with the awakening of the conscious will. A child who has the typical toddler figure for a long time is psychologically not ready for school. Thus, in judging, all these factors should be taken into account. A high rate of failure in the youngest class is related to such unreadiness. Even when a child just manages to cope, and later catches up, his self-confidence will have been dented and this often explains the extremely common feelings of inferiority.

There should really be a dialogue between nursery schools and primary schools, so that the decision on who is ready to move up is made in an understanding manner.

Meanwhile, slightly precocious five and six-year-olds can be a big problem in nursery schools. They are ready for school but cannot start because they have not reached the age of six by the date laid down by law. As long as such matters are dealt with by law and are not left to the responsible judgment of educationalists and school doctors, the only solution is to have separate transition classes in nursery schools. Experience has shown that it does not work for these children to be with others in certain activities, for example, at story-time.

Entering school concludes the first stage of development. In this period we have seen the child as a being who found his place in the world by imitation and developed by means of an invisible inner force, exposing what was already there in embryonic form. This took place in such a way that thinking, feeling and the will appeared one after the other. The following table illustrates this schematically.

Birth to 2 years	Period of sensory perception. Upright position, walking, talking. Baby figure.
From 2 years	Development of *thinking:* association of the content of perception. Transition from baby to toddler figure.
From 4 years	Development of *feeling:* creative imagination. Nursery—schoolchild figure. First growth in breadth.
From 5 ½ years	Development of the conscious *will.* The child is ready for school. Transition towards the figure of the school-age child. First growth in height.

4. From loss of the milk teeth to puberty

Before describing the second seven-year period we shall look at the first year at school. The psychological stage of the child at the age of seven is indicated in the scheme at the end of the previous chapter.

In his thinking he is at the close of a phase which started at two-and-a-half, when he began to name the outside world and make associations. He does not yet have any abstract ideas. The child's feeling is still at the stage of creative imagination, when the world is still covered with the merciful veil of his own imagination. Only the will, which emerges when he starts to set his own goals in the outside world, introduces reality. However, the first goals are still an attempt to achieve certain desires; and as such the drives and the will are still closely related to the physical needs of the child.

This means that he is not yet ready to assimilate abstract concepts, in long lessons at school. There is certainly a difference between the first year at school and nursery school, since the former should be exclusively concerned with the element of play, while the first year at school also takes into account the awakening will. However, this first year should only be slightly different from nursery school, and the transition carefully monitored. The creative imagination and rhythmic element of play should on no account be suddenly broken off. The metamorphosis of these soul forces is an important matter, and is described fully later.

4.1 From seven to nine:
the first metamorphosis of thinking

It is only towards the end of the seventh year of life, when the child moves into his second year at school, that he really enters the new stage. His body has now made the revolutionary change from the figure of a toddler to that of school age child. During the transition period his legs first start to grow and to become more agile. Then the trunk changes, and finally, at about the age of seven the face also undergoes a marked change. It is not only the shape that changes. The change in shape is the result of the growth of the lower jaw which follows the rhythm of growth of the legs. Thus the jaw grows further forward and while, until recently, the lip protruded, the upper and lower lips now come together. Because of the increased length of the lower half of the face the relation between the facial bones and the rest of the skull has changed considerably; the former area is relatively much larger; the sockets of the eyes have become relatively smaller.

Along with the shape of the face the expression changes considerably during the seventh year of life, and reflects the important metamorphosis in the inner life which is taking place in the child's thinking.

It has already been pointed out that the toddler was a single sensory organ, taking in everything around him and assimilating it by imitation. His open expression faced the world full of trust, and his half-closed mouth, always ready to laugh or cry, expressed this in his physiognomy.

The expression of a seven-year-old is quite different. His eyes gaze at the outside world expectantly. His mouth is shut, and there is now a wall between the inside and the outside world, a threshold between the outside world and the child's inner world. His own world is an enclosed, encapsulated area where he feels at home, a sort of operational basis from where he reconnoitres the outside world and takes the knocks inflicted by it.

Thinking is no longer limited to eagerly grasping and associating perceptions of the outside world but is gradually able to stretch its wings and soar in its own element. It acquires the possibility of developing its own images; in other words, the child rises from *perception* to *concepts*. During the first years of the second stage the life in thought-pictures is very pronounced; the images amalgamate to form an enclosed world which is not disrupted until puberty.

This childish world has a strange 'realistic unreality'. All the elements from outside which were incorporated during the previous stage have a place here, but the way they are arranged and combined, and above all, the way in which they are assessed, is new and peculiar to this stage.

Images are not yet sharply defined; they are fluid, mobile and active like people in a stage-play. They are comparable to the day-dreams of adults in which the imagination and drives interact with the images of the individual imagination, quite separately from the outside world of reality. Day-dreaming is the survival in later life of the type of thinking characteristic of this stage of childhood. It may lead to a useless waste of time and even to perversions, but also to the poetic mood in which more of reality is experienced than is possible with plain common sense.

If we are aware of our own day-dreams which may lead to highly poetic experiences we shall also be able to understand the child during this stage, and to help him. To provide the right educational diet for children in the first three years of primary school, we should really be poets. This may sound rather fanciful, but it makes psychological sense.

During the first stage of life the child through his openness and imitation has learned to fit into society. After the age of seven he is much more aware of the speech around him. He wishes the world and its purpose and direction to be recounted and painted in words. He feels attracted to people who can describe images in words, who can be loving and praise him with words, and who can tell really good stories.

During the first stage the child mastered language through imitation and this formed the basis for his thinking. Once again it is language and words that make the metamorphosis of thinking possible, so that it acquires a new character.

The child can only grasp the spoken word and come to understand through speaking. He should be told many things now, but in a particular way; not in prosaic abstraction, but with imagination in active, vibrant stories. Fairy-tales and fables form the right educational diet. The teacher should be a creative and poetic artist with words. This appeals to children and gives them something for the whole of life that can never be taken away. They are not given stones as bread.

The child is not a blank page when he comes to school, for during the first phase of life through imitation he learned morality from the parental environment. What was then initiated should now be carried further by a teacher, and this is only possible through words, in stories and talk. The teacher should not moralize; that produces a sort of 'moral acid' in the child's soul, but he should ensure that the great and small truths of life penetrate the child's inner world artistically and creatively.

As thinking is freed from perception, and becomes

established in a world of its own, memory expands and becomes continuous. The small child's memory has a partial character, only certain events are remembered, usually those with a strong emotional or drive-content. Thus the small child could face life every day with fresh joy. Now he is more concerned with representation than with perception. When he was bound to the here and now, the relationship develops between the representation-image and the memory-image.

He does not immediately notice the loss of paradise. It is only when the emotional life has also undergone metamorphosis that he begins to *experience* his loss.

The first three years of school form a period which may be considered psychologically as a unit. It is a particularly happy period. Everything conspires to place the child in a state of balance and harmony, and this will never recur during the rest of his life. The awakening forces of the will are still greatly influenced by the imagination and eagerly reach out into the expanding world of thought. A whole new world opens up, and the child surrenders to this world with awe. Basically there are no problems of discipline in the first three years at school. The teacher is an unquestioned authority and the child willingly follows the rules. Hence the teacher's responsibility is greater and care of the teaching programme is now all the more important. It is easy enough to carry a child's powers of abstract thought beyond his stage. In particular the precocious children will eagerly learn intellectually. However, the same children have no counterweight in natural country life and for them it is important to awaken and develop the creative forces related to feeling and the will. There is no doubt that the modern system of education fails to fulfil these needs. The premature drying up of these sources of creative force have an almost irreparable influence on the entire unfolding personality, for every subsequent metamorphosis of soul forces must be based on earlier stages.

Any school medical adviser or child psychiatrist looking round at children today must be horrified to note the crippling of the soul life of children. Noteworthy is the difference between city children and country children. The latter have greater reserves to retain more of their natural rhythm in the same educational programme.

A system aimed at producing whole people must in these first three years satisfy and guide the intellectual needs of children in such a way that the forces of the creative imagination are also nourished. Extra lessons need not be added for activities such as story-telling, handicrafts, playing with clay and rhythmic gymnastics, but every hour in school should be permeated with an artistic spirit. This puts great demands on the teachers. But is not the work of the teacher one of the most important in society? To an immeasurable extent teachers determine the society of the next decades.

During the last decades there have been constant complaints that schools produce very few original creative people. There is a terrifying tendency to surrender to the herd instinct and propaganda. This evil can only be attacked at the roots, and these can largely be found in the first three years of the primary school.

Our present system is too much based on *reproducing facts*. Only skill in reproducing facts is fully practised in primary, secondary and higher education. An example is given and has to be copied. The children learn by heart what is written in books. Only the occasional essay written in higher classes calls upon the child's creative skill, which by that time is all too restricted.

Yet it is possible to organize education in a way which ensures that from the very beginning the lessons are inwardly worked upon and digested by the children, and they are not asked merely to rely on memory. It is possible to tell a story about history or geography and then test the children to see if they are capable of reproducing it. However, it can also be tested by asking them to make a drawing of the events in the story that made the greatest impression. It is interesting to see which events are chosen, and how the story has been assimilated. Something taken in aurally can be recreated visually. Similarly, a visual stimulus can be transformed into writing.

This avoids a direct reflection of what was heard or seen, and the child has to relate to the material at deeper levels of his soul. At the same time it is practice for the memory, and the creative forces of feeling and the will are also involved in this new production (not reproduction).

Modern man has become so used to reproduction that as an adult he is often only capable of reproducing the views that are put before him. Is not this one of the causes of the terrible catastrophes taking place all around us? Present-day education must be concerned with the choice between exclusive reproduction or the possibility of drawing out creative and productive skills.

During this stage a normal child gains his own little world with growing enthusiasm; a world still enclosed by the safe walls of the feelings in his own self. Between inner and outer world there is still a coloured veil of imagination. This little world is in many ways comparable to the small principalities of the eighteenth century where the prince or duke could walk around the borders of his own realm before breakfast. However, within those miniature states it was just as busy as in a large one. The princes were concerned with foreign policy and had financial, social and communication problems, just as real as true concerns of the larger states.

The problems of the child's realm are extremely important to him. They are a practice-ground for later 'real' life. Just as the small child needed to practise using his hands, the older child needs material for his whole soul being, and not only for the intellectual powers.

The importance of fairy-tales continues during this period. Initially the child was attracted by the simpler tales, but now the whole of the complicated and differentiated world of reality and fantasy opens up and he lives in the thousands of details and events as though he is looking from an observation post with coloured windows.

Failure to recognize the significance of fairy-tales is evident in the remark made by the mother of a seven-year-old retarded child: 'Now that I see how he still enjoys fairy-tales, I know that he really is retarded.' However, our view was that this was in fact one of the hopeful symptoms for the child's further development. For a seven-years-old a liking for fairy-tales is quite normal. However, many children are *not* told such stories and, *imitating the adults around them,* they learn precociously to despise them.

In addition to fairy-tales the teacher must create his own small artistic tales, expressing the 'big world' with its spring and autumn, sun, clouds and rain, stones, plants and animals, just as they are represented in fables. People with children of their own, or able to recall their own youth, will remember that the best stories are those which the story-teller made up himself. I am still grateful to my uncle who would tell an endless series of stories whenever he came to visit, about 'naughty little Edward': 'Well, children, the things naughty little Edward got up to today ...' He always started his stories like this, as the children sat around eagerly waiting to hear the next instalment.

Thinking continues to follow in its new direction up to puberty. However, changes meanwhile occur in other corners of the child's soul life, disturbing the harmonious state of the first years at school, and therefore also influencing the whole way in which the world is represented.

4.2 From nine to twelve: The metamorphosis of feeling

A significant and this time radical change in the child's relation to the world only occurs when the child moves up in the fourth year at school. Every experienced teacher knows that the fourth year is much more difficult than the three preceding years. In most cases the class has developed into a small community during the first three years, and it is pleasant to teach there. The children believe whole-heartedly in their teacher, the class has an intimate character, and the children work harmoniously and productively. Often such a pleasant class to teach changes at the beginning of the fourth year into an undisciplined, unsettled rabble. The intimacy disappears and the teacher in whom the children believed whole-heartedly only six months earlier is now 'rotten', or 'really nasty'. The child is now nine years old. What happens during the tenth year of his life to make him so moody and intractable, critical of everything and despising fairy-tales as childish?

A complete change seems to have come over his feelings as though he has lost the protection of the imaginative world projected outside himself, as though he suddenly, seeing its worst side, experiences the world as a hostile place.

It is true that the long period of the child's free imagination, which had surrounded him so comfortably, has come to an end. The feelings undergo a great transformation. The change which had occurred in thinking at the age of seven takes place in the tenth year of life with regard to feeling. Feeling becomes more objective; first, in isolated incidents, and later increasingly, the child becomes aware of his loneliness. Semi-consciously he experiences his separateness from the cosmos, his imprisonment in the dark world of his physical being.

Suddenly he is afraid in the dark. He is afraid there might be a man under the bed and crawls right under the blankets, quickly removing his legs from under the bed. The door to the hallway has to be left open, and mother and father have to be able to hear him. Again and again he will try to conquer the fear provoked by the world with magical charms, for example, if when he goes to bed, he coughs loudly before entering the room, or reaches the bed via various rugs without stepping on the floorboards, nothing will happen. Everyone will have their own memories of this period, which may continue into puberty. The child has become critical. The people he respected most and who had been placed on a pedestal, fall the furthest, and this makes the child himself very unhappy. In his unhappiness he will use ever more critical terms. Suddenly he is critical of his immediate surroundings. He will look at his mother long and seriously, then say something like: 'I think your hair looks really stupid, Mum,' without any indication of where this has suddenly come from. It is as if the world which he had always accepted as a matter of course, and which he used to describe proudly to his friends, is now seen for the first time: 'I think our garden is really horrible,' or 'Why is it always so dark in this house in this nasty street?' At first these moods are separated by weeks when everything revives with its former joy and pleasure, but criticism affects everything, and gradually increasingly spoils his open acceptance.

At this time children see very acutely: discord between the parents, formerly ignored is now noticed and experienced as a great sadness. His attitude to death changes. One can be quite surprised by the unconcerned way in which little children view death. Dead is dead, which simply means that the dead are no longer visible and are 'with the angels'. When he is put to bed at night a small child may suddenly ask: 'Does Grandad wear his black hat with the angels too?' only to babble on immediately about the wonderful hole he is digging and which he's going to finish tomorrow. However, at this age death is first seen as a problem and leads to profound pondering.

The child *experiences* himself as being separate from the outside world, which is not as beautiful, amenable or intelligent as that created by his imagination. He grows lonely, and it is a shock to be faced with the dualism of the self versus the world. In the metamorphosis in thinking, dualism was not yet experience, because feeling was still hidden in the protective cloak of childish imagination. However, now this is torn away, and the contrast between self and world, inner and outer, becomes a reality of life. It happens first in the feelings, not yet in the will: the child does not yet draw the consequences of his dualistic philosophy. This is apparent in his intolerance, his indecision and sudden difficult moods, marked swings from content to discontent, and above all, in his opposition to the outside world, though this is still expressed in words and feelings rather than actions. While on the one hand, he finds everything 'boring' and 'stupid', on the other, he is keen for new experiences, like going to places where no one has ever been. His attitude to life is ambivalent and dualism is its leitmotif.

A teacher who wishes to help these children develop as fulfilled adults will be ready for this crisis of the tenth year of life. Before the respect for a single person disintegrates, he will direct it towards the supra-personal character of man. The child must realize that the adored adult himself recognizes a higher authority and lives accordingly. He must experience the authority above his own. But in addition, the child should develop a relationship with nature, and especially discover the place of man in nature, not so much in scientific terms, but at an artistic level. In this way, when he loses the absolute respect for a single person it can be transferred to mankind as a whole with all its human characteristics, in its place amongst stones, plants and animals.

The child's eyes are now open to nature, and his inner needs are met with stories about nature and experiences of the natural world. Drawing leaves and plants is a way of helping him to become familiar with the shapes of nature. He will now seek a new object in the environment for his respect and this feeling should be directed at figures above ordinary human level. The Old Testament and mythology contain a wealth of material for these years, and during the following years history brings the child into contact with heroes who are shining examples in the development of mankind. Respect for such figures evokes the highest forces.

If the need for hero-worship which awakens during

this stage is not properly guided, the child will reach out for idols, and inevitably meet disappointment.

Chapter 7, on the place of the self in the development of the child, shows this crisis of the tenth year to be an extremely important turning point; one that falls into another rhythm of development than that described here.

4.3 Between twelve and fourteen: Pubescence

After the crisis of the tenth year of life there are two or three years before the period usually known as pubescence, when another metamorphosis takes place and the consequences of all that the child has experienced in its feelings become apparent.

Now the total separation of the child's own personality from the outside world begins. It is a metamorphosis of his will in relation to the world.

The child first became involved with the world at school age, by setting himself specific goals and trying to achieve them. Now all his activities are aimed at conquering this outside world as a whole. This process begins in pubescence and is completed during the years of real puberty.

The word 'to conquer' is chosen deliberately, for the child's outer relationships acquire a manifestly aggressive character. Games such as cops and robbers and cowboys and Indians are popular for boys. They like to fight each other, not only when they're quarrelling, but also for the sheer joy of grabbing each other, imposing their will and experiencing their own strength. For boys, girls have become inferior creatures, only good for having their pigtails pulled or being teased in other ways. The boys' movements become clumsy and angular. Agility is lost. It becomes clear only at this stage that small children have the flexibility of natural rhythm and that their actions are

95

based more on the rhythmic elements of play than directed at a goal.

At this age boys like to form gangs for all sorts of possible and impossible reasons: to make a raft and float it together, to build a hut, or simply to seek adventure or fight against other gangs. As the will becomes more conscious, the social element also awakens, because the desire for social structure is always related to the will.

As these forces are released, they should be guided by teachers; otherwise youngsters soon become prone to vandalism. Organizing groups for trekking into the countryside can be an excellent educational way of achieving this. It is very important to make sure that youngsters at this age are not involved in the political egotism of groups.

A boy who is just about to enter puberty should be directed towards the totality of the world, and be taught to find moral strength therein. Countless youth movements have made positive attempts in this direction, but this is still too little when everything is taken into account; and schools themselves will have to deal with these difficulties.

For girls the problems are slightly different. Again there is a tendency to band together in groups, but there is not such an aggressive dominating streak. Girls turn inwards, shutting out the outside world in a rather hostile way by being exclusive in their groups, tending to indulge in mysterious day-dreams, giggling and being difficult and obstinate towards adults.

Up to now we have discussed the development of the 'child', without a distinction between boys and girls, because there was no essential difference. However, now boys and girls must be discussed separately.

The physiological development of girls starts at an earlier age, and this has certain consequences for psychological development. Girls start to mature physically between the ages of thirteen and fourteen, when they suddenly shoot up. During this period a great deal of their strength goes into physical growth. As a result their objective achievements in the outside world are reduced. They suddenly feel less capable of doing things, get tired more quickly, can't join in on bike rides and sports, and this they find quite inexplicable themselves. It is common for girls to suffer from anaemia during this period, and grow so quickly that they have no strength left. Psychologically this leads to a tendency to be bad-tempered and depressed, and to the obstinacy and indecision referred to above. Usually this condition lasts no longer than about a year, then a balance is achieved, growth is no longer so dramatic, and once menstruation has started, the storm is generally over and the usual vital feelings return. However, this is followed by the real period of psychological puberty, discussed later, and should not be confused with the physiological period of depression referred to here.

While girls' physical capacities are reduced at the approach to puberty, the opposite is true for the physical achievements of boys. They are brimming with vitality and need to get rid of their excess energy, either in organized activities or in boisterous high spirits.

It does not help to complain about the high spirits of youngsters, and at this stage schools have to solve the problem in an educational way. Obviously this demands much time from teachers, but good teachers must be able to anticipate and guide this period, because the development of the will brings a fresh emergence of feelings of respect, which are no

97

longer as easily satisfied as when the child was six years old.

The boys' will in relation to the outside world has a realistic-romantic character. An young child may want to be a fire-engine driver because it is such fun to sound the sirens, or a ticket-collector because it is such fun to clip the tickets. A twelve-year-old boy has acquired a realistic understanding of the situation around him. Thus he will seek his ideals further from home. He may want to travel the world and become a pilot, for he imagines that in this way he will be able to escape the constraints of his parental environment and get out in the world. So begins the third great period of development. The first seven-year period brought about a *physiological* development; thinking, feeling and the will emerge from their previous bondage. The second seven-year period of development reveals a *psychological* development. Thinking, feeling and the will are already present but undergo a transformation within the safe confines of the child's own personality. The third period reveals the *social development*. During this period the teenager must learn to relate to the world and start to act from the ground of his inner self. Child development to the age of fourteen is summarized in the table below.

Birth to 2 years	Period of sensory perception Upright position, walking, talking. Baby figure.
From 2 years	Development of *thinking:* association of the content of perception. Transition from baby to toddler figure.
From 4 years	Development of *feeling:* creative imagination. Nursery—schoolchild figure. First growth in breadth.
From 5 ½ years	Development of the conscious *will.* The child is ready for school. Transition towards the figure of the school-age child. First growth in height.
From 7 years	Metamorphosis of *thinking.* Self-contained world of though-images. Schoolchild figure.
From 9 years	Metamorphosis of *feeling.* Awakening criticism. Separation of self and world. Second growth in breadth.
From 11 or 12	Metamorphosis of the *will.* Pubescence. Second growth in height.

5. Development from puberty

During the physical maturation before puberty, the question of sexuality arises in the child's soul. The physical changes which a girl notices taking place in herself and her friends lead to a physiological curiosity which can simply be described as curiosity related to reproduction as such. The onset of menstruation in particular is a milestone in a girl's life, and initially casts a mysterious aureole around the world which the child is entering. The changes are less striking for boys; in the first place they occur a year or two later than in girls and even then the first erection and first ejaculation do not make a great physiological impression. Nevertheless, boys also go through a measure of physiological curiosity when they want to know the way in which sexuality functions.

During this period sexuality is of direct biological interest and the dreams of children of this age are full of undisguised sexual acts and symbols, usually based on organic stimuli. Counsellors often have to deal with many different sorts of 'dirty games', such as cowboys and Indians which end up with girls and boys undressing and looking at each other. As long as these games do not go too far, they are usually of little significance. In most cases the reason for them is that psychological guidance was lacking during this period, and failure to give the children sufficient material for their imagination and activity. Mostly this is simple to deal with: in addition to a mildly serious reprimand, the children should be involved in an enthusiastic plan for some meaningful activity. The worst thing is for the frightened teacher to try and eradicate such 'sins' authoritatively, and thereby transform the child's 'physiological deviation' into a dark area of his life.

Fortunately for children, most of these games are not discovered, and a normal child soon grows out of them once his curiosity has been satisfied. Puberty takes over and then the child is beset by such enormous problems that the earlier curiosity is soon forgotten. Sexuality then continues to be one of several problems for many years, though it is by no means the most important.

Puberty is unjustifiably described as sexual maturity, and this means that one particular aspect of a multi- faceted development is unduly highlighted, so that the whole phenomenon is seen in a wrong perspective. It would be more correct to describe sexual maturity as world maturity, for during this period the child becomes aware not only of the reality of the other sex, but of the reality of the whole world and the distinction between the sexes is but a modest part of this.

Puberty is a wonderfully dramatic event in the life of a child. In *Parsifal* Richard Wagner has written a drama reminiscent of the drama of puberty. When Parsifal, after entering it in the innocence of childhood, was banished from the Castle of the Grail because as the 'pure fool' he did not ask the question, he came into Klingsor's magic garden. Here was a fantastic landscape containing wonderful exotic flowers of every colour. When Parsifal then breaks the enchantment, Klingsor throws a spear at him which he catches in his hand. At that moment a peal of thunder is heard and it suddenly becomes dark. The whole magic world collapses and the next moment Parsifal stands alone in the grey light, surrounded by a pitiless rocky waste-land. In this grey loneliness he must find himself and thus rediscover the path to the Grail Castle.

This reflects the experiences of the onset of puberty. The light colourful child's world of flowers is ripped apart and the youngster suddenly finds himself in a bare grey world of so-called 'naked facts. This moment, which is one of the most dramatic in *Parsifal*, making a deep impression on the audience, is an experience everyone undergoes once in his life.

Loneliness is the leitmotif of puberty. A thought often found in the diaries which are typical is: 'No one understands me. Has anyone ever been as lonely as me?'

The path towards other people — to the community of the Grail, to use the image of *Parsifal* — is sought out of loneliness. After a time of analysis and separation there is a search for synthesis, and this dominates all the efforts made during the seven years before full adulthood. The synthesis between mankind and the world can only be discovered when man finally acquires the strength which is present when two or three people are together in His name, just as in the drama of *Parsifal*.

The characteristic of teenage imbalance is related to the experience of loneliness. Again and again it is a central feature of experience and has shattering strength. It may be temporarily vanquished when the child surrenders to the illusion of the world of childhood, but increasingly this fails him and he must find other ways of combating the dark void of his soul.

The youngster will seek an older friend who understands him in his loneliness and gives him a hand to lead him out of the maze of his conflicting feelings. The phrase 'sexual maturity' suggests that during this period young people will tend to seek

103

refuge most of all with a companion of the same age and opposite sex. Nothing could be further from the truth. Sexuality recedes from its earlier place; boys seek out an older male friend, girls an older girlfriend, to open their heart to and to respect with a new glow. They all seek a friend and leader. Heterosexuality is secondary and homo-erotic tendencies come to the fore. The love for boys in the culture of ancient Greece was an openly recognized educational factor, and the camaraderie of sport, student fraternities and military life are typical of this period.

This passing physiological phase should not be confused with homosexuality, although it cannot be denied that in many cases of 'latent homosexuality' the person concerned has failed to outgrow the period of puberty.

Puberty is a stage when young people start to seek their own place in a much larger world. They are beset with new questions: 'Where am I? Where is my place? How do others see me?' It is a search for identity. If a boy fails to find his own identity, he will either withdraw from society in the years following puberty or 'join the herd' believing that being part of a community presupposes his own value.

The escape into the herd can take all sorts of conflicting forms in particular social conditions, but it is always the consequence of failure to discover an identity.

Another problem is to form a new relation to sexuality which initially appeared in its biological aspects. Some degree of intimacy should be found here. Through intimacy, sex is transformed into *eros*, a personally experienced force in interrelationships. If this activity is not fulfilled, this leads to loneliness and alienation *vis-à-vis* the other sex, but also in other social relationships, such as at work and with friends.

As a result of intimacy the outside world is again experienced as an inner world to which the self can relate.

Authority as an educational principle no longer applies with the onset of puberty. The young person wishes to acknowledge older people as leaders through friendship. A great deal of the misery of family life is caused by parents retaining their authoritarian attitude when their children have reached puberty and they do not succeed in guiding them in friendship. Quite rightly the child now experiences authority as an insult to his personality.

During the first seven years the child was still one with the world and the world still formed part of his being; during the second period of seven years the self and the world gradually separate and at the age of fourteen the loneliness of puberty is upon him.

The new relationship between the self and the world which is sought after should be a fully conscious relationship established by the young person himself.

5.1 Boys from fourteen to sixteen: Looking for an view of the world

The first area in which a synthesis is sought is in thinking. Thinking is activated and the child seeks for a world image in which the self is placed within the total cosmos.

For the boy who looks outward during this period the whole world, and even the whole universe and all that it contains, becomes a vast area for endless voyages of discovery. Depending on his level of development his interests may be narrow or extremely varied.

In the first place a boy at this age will plunge into the world of technology. He will be knowledgeable about things like computers with an astonishing amount of self-confidence when such fields still contain so many secrets for the older generation. He can build a working radio set just like that, soon learns everything there is to know about engines and after a while starts to find small repairs at home quite childish.

Most boys also have a great need to understand the secrets of the cosmos. They look forward to the subject of cosmography, and I remember my own disappointment when this subject at school turned out to consist of computing angles between imaginary lines.

In this way a boy develops a view of the world rooted in the sciences as presented by our culture. It totally satisfis him at this age and he can relate to the enthusiasm of the scientists who contributed to it during the second half of the nineteenth century.

Boys also enjoy reading books about discovery of distant lands, and every boy goes through a stage when he wants to become an explorer, and in fact is an explorer on his holiday trips. This is the age too when he wants to become a pilot or a sailor, when the room is a web of electric wire, and an old car battery is his most treasured possession. He will experiment with a perseverance which is never seen at school, and hope and failure are the two poles of his life. There are two main areas of interest: a large group favours science and technology, and a smaller group is interested in literature and humanitarian questions. Both groups might start magazines and write articles.

Thus, for example, I came across a monthly magazine that was published in three typewritten versions and was available on subscription, and had the ambitious title: *Physica et Natura - A monthly magazine for the natural sciences and biology.* The articles, all written by three friends aged fourteen and fifteen, revealed the typical characteristics of puberty. There were serials taken from the biographies of famous inventors, articles explaining the principles of neon and X-rays, as well as essays on mushrooms and wild plants.

It had all been put together with enthusiasm and a great deal of energy, but was still entirely in the style of a school essay, rather like an encyclopaedia, and lacking any literary feeling. This encyclopaedic taste, the enthusiasm for knowledge and an understanding of facts as such is typical of late puberty.

In other secondary school magazines literary essays predominated, though these were usually written by the same small group. I remember that at this age I would have to write under four different pseudonyms to fill up the various columns as 'editor' of our school magazine.

Among the six hundred or so pupils there were not even half a dozen with enough literary talent to be persuaded to publish their efforts. Yet it is a fact that far more than one per cent have literary creative gifts, as will become clear in the discussion of diaries.

Although knowledge is a popular element in modern life, and boys who are becoming mature gradually form an image of their place in the world, their deepest feelings are by no means satisfied by the widening horizons. Their thinking and insights have ready answers to all sorts of questions and so they can also get carried away by feeling and enthusiasm. However, the experience of man's relationship to his immediate environment has not yet changed. Youngsters are constantly aware of the gap separating them from their fellow creatures; there is still incomprehension about their own self and an inability to express this in any way.

A lonely tender heart beats under the external bravado and quietly wonders at the injustice of the lost paradise of childhood or fiercely rebels against the world, which is hard and sharp and can inflict pain mercilessly.

As a result a young boy is uncertain in his social contacts, like a lobster which has crawled out of its shell to grow a new shell and is temporarily totally vulnerable. Girls have suddenly become a complete mystery. They are hateful, acting with haughty superiority, which he finds unbearable. He blushes and stutters at the most embarrassing moments; in fact, there is no more helpless creature than a strapping lad of fifteen.

However, he feels safer amongst his friends, discussing topics of common interest or competing in sports. But where will he find his one real friend, a friend who will totally understand, to whom he can bare his feelings and who will say the right word with gentle humour and real love when he is searching for new truths about life? He will believe he has found this friend, but is disappointed, and in fact he should be disappointed because friendship can only endure when there is a reciprocal capacity for giving, and a fifteen-year-old has only uncertainties to give. What he shows outwardly is always different from what he really feels.

Even so, a strange and tender love can also develop at this age for a girl who is adored at a distance. This love has no sexual content, for that is felt to be sacrilegious. The object of his love is adored as a distant madonna, a fleeting encounter may suffice for weeks, the girl may not know anything about it, while the boy suffers deeply for this simple romantic idea. Everything is veiled with a slight melancholic haze, even the moments of greatest ecstasy. This is the indeterminate desire for the blue flower of the romantics.

This does not conflict with the possibility that a boy

may 'go out' quite openly with a girl at other times. To impress his friends he must act in an adult way, talk about sex and have a girl. This is part of the discovery of the world in all its aspects, but the innermost depths are rarely reached in this fashionable amorous camaraderie, a product of the twentieth century which is as much an aspect of fashion in some classes or clubs as wearing a particular hat or scarf.

Amid all these conflicting feelings and impulses the boy is unable to talk about his deepest desires, because the person before him makes him aware of his own shortcomings and the ridiculous aspects of his unspoken longings.

The diary is a product of the soul's dire need, and is as characteristic of puberty as building and drawing are for toddlers. Diaries are a part of puberty; girls start diaries between the ages of twelve and thirteen and often continue up to the age of nineteen or twenty, while boys begin at between thirteen and fourteen and usually stop earlier. The zenith of diary-keeping is between sixteen and eighteen for boys and between fifteen and seventeen for girls.

Although diaries start during puberty, they are as yet mainly an outlet for the child's despair. An invisible friend does not argue and listens with great patience. It takes the place of the real friend who cannot be found, but who may be found in the youngster's future life. The diary is also written for that person. Invisible eyes are upon the paper as the child writes his diary; these are the eyes of the higher self, of the only real guide in life who is still being sought outside and will only be found in the self much later. This awareness of the proximity of the self without finding it, and the inability to find the other person, causes the intense loneliness expressed in the diary.

5.2 Boys between sixteen and eighteen: Religious aspirations

When they reach the zenith of the diary period both boys and girls have got over the real phase of puberty and their feeling now seeks a synthesis with the world. As a result the diary acquires a very different character. The artistic element starts to outweigh the record of events and effusions of feelings. Short poems, rhythmic prose and essays describe experiences of nature, vague religious feelings and love of distant objects result in further creations the less love is requited. A keen girl-friend now seldom inspires a fiery sonnet.

If the young person's view of the world grows in the following years and he finds a place for himself, his endeavour to achieve a synthesis may descend into the deeper layers of his soul life and finally be realized there.

The youth's picture of the world, shaped by his environment, has only clearly shown him that he is cut off from the other people and from a higher spiritual world. The twentieth-century world-view reveals man as an insignificant grain of sand in an infinite world; in this outlook, however, the soul cannot survive. Therefore the synthesis of self and world now becomes the relation between self and other people, self and society, self and God.

This feeling was present before in the duality which often failed to become conscious, appearing first in the restlessness at the age of nine or ten. During puberty the irrepressible intensity could lead to depression and in some cases even to suicide.

The formation of a world-view is followed at the age of sixteen or seventeen by a search for a religious relation to other people and to God. This quest can take many forms, some of which may even have an aggressive, anti-religious content, even though they are religious! It emerges in society or through the failed encounter in the herd, or often even in the communal experience of nature, camp-fires or singing. The self is only content when it relates to other selves; the youngster who has been involved with himself for so long is now looking for a feeling of belonging.

There is an increasing need of doing things with others, a joy in the sense of community resulting from consciously shared experience; this deepens and strengthens the person's own experience. However, it is a very weak foundation for lasting community and disillusionment often occurs. The sense of inner security often fades after a holiday, a camp or discussion, and leads to a longing for another meeting, another temporary support. This is why the young enjoy coming together so often to discuss or do the same things every time.

Adults may be disappointed to see how unproductive these many meetings are; the young people would rather talk and listen to each other than solve problems. In fact, they reject suggested solutions, for solutions mean that further discussion is no longer necessary, and the whole point is to come together, search together and keep searching. Anyone who realizes this, understands that the hot air covers a burning desire to belong to a community, will have the patience to nourish this spirit unobserved, at the same time providing building stones for a true and deeper communal sense. That can only mature in the course of years when a person has gained his own relationship to the nature of that giving, epitomized in the offering of Christ and made possible as a foundation of a true Christian culture.

111

In this active religious seeking immediately following puberty, the religious ideal is sought and experienced with an intense and absolute purpose, a natural inner drive which never recurs in life. Even the most hardened materialist will often smile in recalling this period when religion and poetry could still move 'his youthful spirit'.

For many others these years bring a stormy awakening of philosophical values which accompany them for life, but only become true personal values as life unfolds. For yet others it is an age of romanticism when tournaments are fought and dragons killed for the sake of elusive maidens, as in the Middle Ages.

5.3 Between eighteen and twenty-one: Preparing for a career

If youngsters complete their secondary education they must decide on a career at the age of eighteen, and the development towards full adulthood coincides with the first steps needed. In preparing for a career the young person enters society with his *will*. This now undergoes its final transformation. It is borne by the world-view that has been formed, the ideals that have been awakened. The young person acts out his ideals, supported by his will, and feels responsible for the emerging social structure.

5.4 Girls after puberty

It has already been pointed out that girls mature physiologically at an earlier age than boys. While puberty in boys coincides with physiological puberty, taking place roughly between fourteen and sixteen, the two are separate in girls. Physiological or sexual maturing takes place between twelve and fourteen, while psychological maturing only comes between fourteen and sixteen, the difficult 'teenage years'.

While the boys during this period turn eagerly to the outside world, in puberty girls are concerned with experiencing the human soul. They become completely involved in human relationships, the stirrings of feeling. They understand, sympathize and empathize with all human life around them, and without restraint declare their own feelings about the confusion they meet in the world. In addition, they experience loneliness, as much and probably even more intensely than boys. Boys live between two poles: their own loneliness and they joy in understanding the world. Girls remain much more preoccupied with their own experience, because the world which they are trying to grasp is the human soul.

Physically mature, with an astonishing insight and intuition into human relations, but without the support of her own or a focal point to serve as a resting-place — just as boys do, the girl will seek a friend of her own sex to be a confidante so that her loneliness can be momentarily relieved. She is vulnerable, over-sensitive, emotional and desperate, alternately ecstatic and sobbing uncontrollably, wise and foolish, outwardly self-assured and inwardly full of doubt, sharing feelings intensely, but nevertheless utterly lonely. This constitutes the psychology of the teenage girl.

Girls have even fewer words than boys to express their feelings. In utter loneliness they can only write about the concerns of their hearts, entrusting them to the silent paper. Even more girls than boys keep diaries, in a literary and creative way. They need to record their experiences with nature and their human encounters, because they feel subconsciously that these inner matters are important. A boy will also do this from time to time, but at other times will consider it to be 'soft'; the boy's self-analysis competes strongly with the vitality of his enthusiasms.

Because of the way they develop, girls become adult more rapidly than boys. A girl of sixteen or seventeen is more mature and is conscious of her superiority as a person. By comparison, a sixteen or seventeen-year-old boy is an awkward baby; when girls are with boys of the same age they are actually leaders, and their generosity in taking any notice of the boys is paid for with all sorts of services. Girls are capricious and constantly want to be pleased, and in their friendships with boys will never allow a hint of their own insecurity to show.

A girl also experiences a deepening of feeling at the age of sixteen or seventeen. The young girl already knew many things which she had not experienced herself, but now she actually experiences these things. Her religious feelings are deep and serious and not easily distracted. The knowledge gained in earlier years becomes wisdom, which means that she can take on tasks which boys are by no means mature enough to do. Nevertheless, it would be wrong to consider an eighteen-year-old girl as being completely adult in a social sense. Although she is more mature and sensitive than a boy of the same age, her endeavours and idealism are not yet down to earth. She must still undergo the last transformation of the will when her ideals are tested and are realized in the social sphere. At this stage the girl must catch up in fields passed by boys in earlier years, and this continues to be the weakness of the female psyche. Throughout their lives women judge the outside world by their own experience, while men are inclined to put their scientific and social insights first.

The social injustice which results in immature girls being used as cheap labour, to be replaced after a few

Birth to 2 years	Period of sensory perception Upright position, walking, talking. Baby figure.

Physiological maturation:

From 2 years	Development of *thinking:* association of the content of perception. Transition from baby to toddler figure.
From 4 years	Development of *feeling:* creative imagination. Nursery—schoolchild figure. First growth in breadth.
From 5 ½ years	Development of the conscious *will.* The child is ready for school, Transition towards the figure of the school-age child. First growth in height.

Psychological maturation:

From 7 years	Metamorphosis of *thinking.* Self-contained world of though images. Schoolchild figure.
From 9 years	Metamorphosis of *feeling.* Awakening criticism. Separation of self and world. Second growth in breadth.
From 11 or 12	Metamorphosis of the *will.* Pubescence. Second growth in height.

Social maturation:

From 14 years	Synthesis of *thought.* World-view. Sexual maturity.
From 16 years	Synthesis of *feeling.* Religious inclination. Third growth in breadth.
From 18 years	Synthesis of the *will.* Social responsibility. Preparing for a career. Continuing to mature to manhood or womanhood.

years by other groups of young girls, should be seen from this point of view. Directly following the years when the girl should be forming her world-picture she often starts work, or worse, is unemployed. What view can arise in this situation, in young women who must bring up the families of the future? It can only be one of the injustices and exploitation, for youngsters see such things clearly, if subconsciously, and again subconsciously they form harsh judgments.

These girls have outgrown their families and are used to spending their own money. But they feel a deep resentment because they sense that they were unable to develop during years of great significance for the rest of life. Their only purpose now is to find a partner as quickly as possible, but the damage has been done to the mother of the new family, and the next generation is deprived of the confidence and joy which are necessary in the first years of life.

This educational injustice kindles class resentments. Employed or unemployed they young may quite rightly sense that they were short-changed in their development, and that no courses later on can ever make up for what was missed in earlier years.

This brings us to a matter of far-reaching social importance. The introduction of mechanization and computerization which replace all repetitive work, leaves time for people to think about themselves and discover that they were only allowed a part of their real development.

The employee may ask for other things, but in reality he or she wishes to be a whole person, and for this the question of education of the adolescent should be thoroughly reviewed, not simply by adding more classes where the same old subjects are repeated, but by a whole new system of education based on the psychological needs of the respective phases.

6. The layers of the human soul

The scheme at the end of the last chapter can also be drawn up in a different way. It is possible to compare the psychological development of a child with that of a plant. The plant grows from a simple form, the seed; the stem shoots up, forming crowns of leaves at various levels, finally producing a flower and fruit. As each new leaf develops higher up, the previous lower ones continue to exist, completely preserving their function. The growth is focused on the tip, where the new organ will appear; those already there continue to function, supporting the growth of the new organ; otherwise, when the function is fulfilled the organ partially dies off.

The flower can only develop when the leaves have unfurled and established their nutritional function; the fruit can only grow when the flower has served its purpose and the reproductive organs form the basis of the new fruit and seed. In The *Metamorphosis of Plants* Goethe describes the living organism in its rhythmic pattern of expansion and contraction. The seed is the most compact form of the plant. The germinating plant expands, growing leaf after leaf, each larger and more beautiful. This is the first form in which the plant appears. It is followed by a contraction; the leaves become smaller and the flower starts to develop on the stem. A strong contraction of the leaf becomes visible in the calyx, and then the leaves once again unfold in the petals. This is the plant's second revelation. The petals are leaves, but compared with green leaves, they have undergone a great transformation. Yet another extreme contraction of the leaf takes place in the stamens. The ovaries then swell up to form the fruit enclosing the seed as a third expansion. The seed develops in the fruit as the third and last contraction of the plant. Leaf, flower and fruit are the three successive stages of leaf- development.

The plant emerges at three levels, each with a metamorphosis of the leaf, each level separated by a contracted form. In the same way man grows to adulthood in three stages, each a metamorphosis or further development of the previously evident stage.

The adult always gains nourishment from the hidden layers of the soul. His deepest world-view and confidence in life are rooted in the first stage of existence, and he uses the forces arising during the second stage in his emotional as well as in his artistic life. As a conscious person he builds on the foundations laid during the third stage.

Anyone who is aware of this will constantly feel the enormous responsibility of parents and teachers towards the next generation. The basis for a sense of trust in life is laid by the parents, who guide the first stage of development.

School, which is largely responsible for the forming of the second period, lays the foundations for our later feelings and the joy we can experience in artistic creation.

The third stage is only realized in a small proportion of the population; a child who starts work at sixteen must simply make the most of any chances that come along.

These are three vital issues facing our society which must be answered.

Parents will have to seek ways to strengthen the foundations of their own moral and religious life.

Schools will have to introduce an artistic and creative element into education.

Society will have to provide better vocational training.

In a plant development is annual and next year the three successive stages begin anew. In human beings real life only begins when the three stages of development have been completed.

Adults live through three metamorphoses of soul forces, and although they may believe they are merely building on the last of these, it has been shown that the earlier 'levels' also continue to have an influence.

A great deal has been said about the different layers of man's soul life. From observing the sick it has been concluded that there must be deeper layers in which a person subconsciously continues to experience events that took place in his youth. This may then be referred to vaguely as the unconscious or subconscious.

The period of the *first seven years* of physiological

119

development when the child was still entirely connected to life processes and the world around him, survive in adulthood as the *deepest unconscious layer*. The experiences and events of this period live on as though in a deep and dreamless sleep.

The period of the *second seven years* of psychological development survives as the *semi-conscious or subconscious layer*. The experiences and world-view of this period live on as a subconscious dream state.

The period of the *third seven years of* social development remains as a third *totally conscious layer*. The adult continues to build on the experiences and philosophy developed during this period and believes that the previous stages of development have disappeared. It is possible for these previous stages of development to surface, on the one hand, in abnormal and pathological conditions, but on the other hand, also through conscious exercise.

In Chapter 4 the consciousness of the six to nine-year-old child was compared to the daydreams of adults. The more clearly one observes the nature of consciousness of children during the second stage of development, the more similarities will be found with the dreams of adults.

In dreams everything seems more real to inner experience than in waking consciousness; in dreams dramatic feeling overrules logic and reason. The imagery of dreams is derived from the perceptions of daily life, though the dynamic of events in dreams follows dramatic laws influenced by emotion. Everything is expressed in imagery and the real background of the dream must be interpreted through this imagery.

It is possible to draw up a range of dreams, starting with body (or organic) dreams in which the image is caused by bodily organs, continuing with wish-fulfilment dreams, which have their basis in drives, through to those which are images of developmental problems of the soul, and finally prophetic dreams in which the image penetrates a world beyond time and space.

Organic causes, drives, development of the soul, and the spiritual world may all be represented in the dream garbed in imagery taken from the world of perception.

A similar range can be drawn up for the child's imagery during the second stage of development. It can also be found in fairy-tales. There are simple fairy-tales in which the image expresses body processes, for example those in which death and rebirth are related to stages of growth, such as the loss of the milk teeth and puberty.

Other fairy-tales are closer to the development of the soul, for example where three brothers attempt to do something and the youngest, who is described as a good for nothing, succeeds where his older brothers fail. The case of the youngest brother is an image for the will, the 'youngest' of the three soul-forces: thinking, feeling and the will. This theme is particularly common in Norwegian folk tales.

Finally there are fairy-tales about the origin of man in a spiritual world, his descent to earth, his imprisonment in human form and his ultimate release. This theme is most beautifully expressed in Snow White.

It is difficult for an adult to experience the consciousness of the first stage. The reason is that the processes of the body continue quite unconsciously, and at most reveal themselves 'one level higher' in the images of dreams. The roots of our will lie in this world of sleeping unconscious, so that they are not open to our perception. This sleeping world can only be approached through powerful inner concentration excluding any form of intellectual thinking.

6.1 The development of the soul and of the body

Every metamorphosis in thinking coincides with an important change in the appearance of the head and the expression of the face.

The periods of the changes in feeling correspond to the periods of growth in breadth of the trunk.

The critical periods in the development of the will coincide with moments of growth in height, when the limbs in particular grow much longer.

We now attempt a further understanding of the relationship between the psychological rhythm of development and the growth rhythms of particular organs.

A great obstacle to detached observation is the conviction that has been drummed into us that the soul activities of thinking, feeling and the will are centred in the brain. This idea is based on the discovery of so-called 'motor centres' in the brain, which allegedly control the movement of the muscles, and the discovery of centres in the brain-stem, which, if damaged, lead to great changes in a person's emotional make-up.

Although these facts cannot be disputed anatomically, there is the fundamental question whether the organ concerned evokes the psychological function, or whether the latter influences the organ. In other words, which is first, the organ or the psychological function?

The first function to be considered is thinking, and there is not much argument about pointing to the brain as the organ of thinking. (Therefore either the brain gives rise to thinking or thinking uses the brain to manifest.) The task of thinking is to understand creation in its overwhelming complexity and diversity. For this purpose, it attempts to order the multiplicity of perceptions and discover a regular pattern or laws in them.

For example, mathematics only makes sense as the basis of natural laws if there is a mathematical system concealed within the laws themselves, if mathematics is really a creative principle existing outside subjective human thinking.

Man has arrived at a knowledge of particular principles of mathematics and logic by means of thinking. The aim of thinking can only be to become ever clearer and more conscious of reality. Human thinking should increasingly approach divine mathematics and logic, divine thinking, the 'Holy Spirit'. If thinking were subjective and only true for the individual concerned, and not beyond, it would be a waste of time and it would be more sensible to give up thinking altogether.

In order to understand the objective laws of creation through thinking, man is endowed with an instrument in the central nervous system that can be refined to such an extent with constant practice that it is increasingly capable of understanding divine logic. Thinking uses an organ that allows this.

However, not only the activity of thinking has objective reality as a creative principle, but also feeling and the will. The will in its cosmic aspect as a spur to action and change is the opposite of thinking, which investigates natural laws and what *has* happened.

In human beings we find the drive to inner movement and change in metabolism, and outward movement and change in locomotion. The organs in which these creative principles are anchored are those concerned with the metabolic processes, and muscles are the organs of movement. The urge to move is

123

primarily centred in those organs. Psychologically this drive manifests as a need or desire: the need to eat, the reproductive urge, and the desire to move. These rise up from the organic functions of the metabolic reproductive and locomotive organs and are the deepest roots of the will. They only become conscious *will* when the drive combines with regulating conscious thinking.

Thinking as such cannot impel the will, but is merely a regulator, transforming a drive into will. The drive for movement exists even where there is no central nervous system, in plants and the lower animals. Therefore the will cannot be seated in the so-called motor area of the brain. Its origin is primarily based in the organs of movement themselves, and its regulation and control is carried out with the help of the central nervous system. Therefore there is an increased drive to movement when there is a spurt of growth in the limbs, and this is only transformed into will during the course of the years (as in the periods from five to seven and from twelve to fourteen years of age).

The transformation of a blind drive to conscious will is the problem of morality. Thinking, considers what has become, what is past; the will, aimed at what is to come, is always concerned with the future.

With regard to feeling, man is squarely placed in the present. Feeling combines the antithesis of thinking and the will. Therefore, feeling always swings between two poles: sympathy and antipathy, love and hate, friendship and enmity, being open and being reserved, accepting and rejecting.

However, this polarity is a creative principle that permeates the entire cosmos; it is manifest in great and small rhythms taking place in creation.

Rhythm has the singular quality of encompassing

both movement (will) and natural laws (thinking). Rhythm is movement according with natural laws. It has form, not a form in space, but a form in time.

The cosmic rhythms are manifest in the year through summer and winter and in the alternation of day and night. These rhythms, in which certain opposing states alternate, also occur in living organisms in which certain processes occur in rhythmic succession.

Rudolf Steiner pointed out that the normal rhythms of respiration and circulation are not arbitrary, but reflect the great cosmic rhythms of our solar system. Creation and the living organism are related in many ways. The fundamental law of rhythm is systole and diastole (contraction and relaxation), breathing in and breathing out, approaching and going away. Feeling follows the same laws and rhythmically swings between sympathy (approaching, assimilating, breathing in) and antipathy (leaving, rejecting, breathing out). Ecstasy is followed by depression, and domination by liberation.

The rhythm of the life-organs in the range from single-celled creatures to the higher organisms, are respiration, circulation and the rhythmic organs of the digestive system. However, as life-rhythm is a quality of each cell, finer rhythms can be found in all the organs.

When someone is said in popular terms to be warm-hearted or to have a heart of gold, this description may unconsciously contain a great deal of truth. Of course, we do not wish to argue that we feel with our heart and lungs. Anatomically the heart serves to circulate the blood and the lungs are for respiration. However, the rhythm of diastole and systole operating in heart, stomach and intestines and in respiration, provides the foundation of our feelings, and thus a relationship between the feelings and these rhythms lasts throughout our lives. They are not regulated by the central nervous system but by the sympathetic nervous system. In childhood especially, feelings and the rhythms of respiration and circulation are closely connected, and in so far as conclusions may be drawn in this field, it seems that this interrelationship only decreases after the age of nine or ten, when circulation and respiration become more stable and are affected only by strong feelings. When you tell young children a story, you can see that their breathing and pulse fluctuate with moments of tension and relief in the story.

Our views are based on the initial psychophysical relationship between thinking and the central nervous system, feeling and the rhythm of certain organs, mainly located in the chest, and the will and the organs of locomotion, mainly represented in the limbs.

The divine principle of Three in One, which we know as the Father, the Son and the Holy Spirit, is reflected in the human trinity of thinking, feeling and will, and represented in the body in schematic terms by the head, the heart and the limbs.

These points of view are of direct practical significance to educationalists. Just as the teaching of mathematics is aimed at developing logical thinking, gymnastics and sports serve to develop the will. This idea is held particularly strongly in Britain. However, children's games also serve to form the will and when such play is actually aimed at a particular goal, it signifies that the conscious will is awakening; before this stage play was still related to rhythmic functions. This new development in play coincides with a spurt in the growth of the limbs.

In education it is desirable that the will develops

directly through the limbs and not through the head, that is it should be exercised in activities performed with the arms and legs. When children learn their tables by clapping or stamping them, they learn them at an earlier age and better than if they are forced to learn them sitting still. In that case the inhibited drive for movement erupts in acts of vandalism once they get out of school. In music when will is linked with a feeling for the beat, it helps to keep time by tapping with the feet.

Rudolf Steiner proposed in his treatises on education that it would be interesting to observe the correlations between the development of the organs and the child's psychological development. On the basis of the idea of the threefold human organism he described how thinking is only developed when the nervous system and the head have achieved a certain degree of completion; how feeling develops when the rhythmic organs are stabilized, and how the will only matures when the limbs have finished growing. In addition, the important idea emerged that the soul forces of thinking, feeling and the will, are transformed organic forces, which are released as psychological activities when they are no longer needed for the growth and development of the organs.

For many years these ideas have been tested in practice. We tried to answer the question whether it was possible to relate the emergence of particular psychological activities to the child's physical development, as this becomes manifest. It was clear that the emergence of psychological functions occurs in stages, and that these are always accompanied by certain organic changes, outlined in the previous chapters.

In my work with difficult and abnormal children it was often possible to predict the absence or emergence of a particular stage of psychological development from the physical state; and vice-versa: the physical condition of particular organic systems could be found from the psychological development. In other words, it was necessary for certain organic systems to achieve a particular stage of development before the accompanying psychological functions could emerge.

It is not possible to deal with the matter in greater detail here. The facts assembled here show that a psychological function started when the change in an organ group had been largely completed.

The part of the body which first stops growing is the head. It had a 'head start'. By the age of two the circumference of the head is almost 50 cm (20") and after this it only grows another 6 cm (2") in circumference, which is very little in diameter. By comparison the legs grow from a length of 38 cm (15") at the age of two to 88 cm (35") in an adult; more than twice the length. In relative terms the head is finished first. After the age of two, thinking emerges as an activity. At this age, the child's figure becomes that of the toddler in which the large abdomen is the main feature. Passing beyond the toddler-figure, in the fourth year of life the child's creative imagination begins to emerge. When he is five his legs start to grow, and once this process has become so clear that the whole figure of the toddler has changed, the child's will emerges. His relation to the world is different and he is ready for school.

During the seventh year the head and the features change markedly in proportion and expression. New thought processes emerge, enabling the child to begin thinking in images. This is followed by the period from eight to ten when changes again occur in the trunk, and at the age of ten there is a change in the child's feelings which results in the crisis of the ten-year-old.

Puberty begins with the marked growth of the limbs, and this is followed by the change in the will, so that the child is now ready to face the world.

The second stage of puberty brings a harmonization and change in the facial features. The child now views the world with an open face, and tries to form a world picture. This is followed by a time in which the characteristically long thin figure of the period becomes more rounded. This is the age for religious enquiry, a new activity in the feelings. Finally, there is the last stage of maturation; in men this means that the whole skeletal and muscular systems become heavier; in women there is only a slight indication of this process, and it may seem that the previous stage of growth in breadth is continued, although there are also changes in the woman's frame, in the pelvic girdle. This difference coincides with the psychological distinction between man and woman.

7. Development of the self

In the previous chapters the development of the child was described in three periods, each a metamorphosis of the preceding one. In this way an image of the development arose comparable with that of a plant, which also develops in three stages. We recall the idea put forward in the introduction, that man is a creature rooted in two worlds: the physical world of his body, and the divine spiritual world. The time has now come to focus attention on the forces which affect the child's development from the centre of his self. We can show this again schematically below.

Up to now we have been more concerned with the influences on the spirit coming from the body, from 'below'; therefore it is now necessary to deal with those which are manifest in the spirit and come from above.

The part which forms our inner core, and which tells us that we are a particular individual, is the 'self'. We shall first consider how the self is manifest in the soul during the three periods.

When we ask whether consciousness of 'self' has always existed, it is clear that in every individual's development there is a certain moment at which awareness of his own 'self' first became apparent. It is usually a dramatic event in a child's life, when an event is first experienced as belonging to him. It is the moment when the individual first become conscious of his self.

7.1 Self-awareness (age three)

Normally this moment occurs in the third year. Before this time the child has undergone many experiences. He speaks, reacts and does many things which reveal his soul life, but is not yet conscious of his own self. He does not yet relate events to himself as a continuous entity in the flow of time.

The moment at which this self-awareness or consciousness of self awakens can be observed by an outsider. Until this time the child refers to himself by name, 'Johnny' or 'Peter' just as he has learned to name other people and objects. This shows that he does not yet make a distinction between himself and all the other objects and activities which can be identified with a word or a name. Then he becomes aware that his own self is slightly different from anything else in the world. The division between the self and the world has started to come about. Suddenly the child will surprise people around him by saying: 'I want jam,' when the previous day he had still said: 'Johnny wants jam.'

This moment when the child first uses the word 'I' is a milestone in his development; the first memory of events relating to the self also dates from the period when he first used the pronoun 'I'.

Together with the awakening self-consciousness bringing division between the self and the rest of the world, there is a sudden tendency to say 'no' to the outside world. Self-consciousness develops at this time by pushing against the world and opposing it. Scheler characterized man in that he has a self and the ability to say no. With the tendency to say 'no' to everything, which suddenly emerges between the second and third birthdays, comes a period of obstinacy. Usually it lasts a few months, until the self sufficiently sure of its own existence, even when not opposing the world outside.

It is amusing to watch a small toddler suddenly changing. 'I not wee-wee, I not do wee-wee, I not want wee-wee,' he will call out, desperately pressing his legs together.

This obstinate phase is trying for parents who must carry on with normal life using a great deal of patience and tact, and without unnecessarily provoking the child. The only way is to distract his attention from the object of contention, and only when it is absolutely necessary should one insist on a disputed course of action knowing it will result in a scene.

Realizing that this is only a passing phase and feeling delight in the emergence of the child's self will help parents to get through this period, for it is precisely by opposing the outside world that the child is exercising his self- consciousness. It is a general law of sensory psychology that consciousness only exists where resistance is experienced: we can only feel our skin when pressure is applied externally.

As long as we float along on the stream of external

events we do not develop a strong consciousness of self; this can only arise when we see ourselves as individuals outside the event. Adults can do this either by acting against the outside world or by forming an independent opinion. A small child can only act and say: 'Me not go to bed.'

In opposing these normal events the child finds that it has a self and does not simply have to do what is required by the outside world. An experienced observer will be able to tell the difference between normal reactions of discontent and the opposition of this period of obstinacy, wherein suddenly the child is against *everything* which he used to enjoy in the past.

During the years following this phase the consciousness of self develops in two ways: in the first place it gradually becomes more continuous and is not merely asserted at particular moments, and in the second place, there is a shift from outward action against the world to the inner activity of forming an opinion about the world.

By the sixth year these processes have so far developed that the child is ready for school. Some continuity of self-consciousness is essential for learning, and at this stage the child starts developing his own views. Nevertheless, even at a later age the first reaction to any criticism of the self is a primitive reaction of opposition.

Everyone is familiar with the feeling: 'I won't let him get away with that, I'll get him.' The next step is to form a quiet opinion about the situation; to do this the self must be placed outside the events as a detached observer.

The last consideration clearly shows that consciousness of self continues to unfold — or at least should —

from its first emergence at the age of three until old age.

The term 'consciousness of self' expresses manifestation of the self in consciousness. As such, it is a function related to our conscious thinking.

7.2 Experience of self (9 - 10 years)

The self is not only manifest in consciousness, but experienced and felt directly. This experiencing is deeper than the consciousness of self; it is rooted in deeper levels of the soul and is directly connected with our feelings. It is also present when we are not consciously concerned with the self.

The experience of self as a deep-seated reality emerges when the child is ten, is reinforced during pubescence and becomes the dominant feeling in puberty itself. During these years he is aware of his own self, separated from the outside world, and he experiences this as a profound tragedy. Childhood is seen as a lost paradise; he was still safely sheltered in the secure world of family, friends and school. Now the self is naked and unprotected in a strange world.

The first experience of self coincides with the crisis of the nine-year-old, described earlier, which appears in a particular perspective, often highlighting the conflicts that arise. Again the awakening leads to action against the outside world, though this time it occurs in the domain of feelings. The unquestioned respect for teachers disappears and is replaced by for the people around him. Only after many years is this critical faculty turned inwards upon a self which is gradually found to be 'quite hopeless' and this leads to a deep-rooted unhappiness.

This painful experience of self is only conquered after puberty by a new manifestation, this time in the will. This drive can accurately be called the will for self-realization.

7.3 Self-realization (18 years)

After the consciousness of self and the experience of self, a need arises for self-expression to the world, and this happens in terms of what is achieved, for instance in the profession or course of study chosen. A person expresses himself in his life history, in that he acts in the stream of time.

The breakthrough to realization of the self implies a release from the fruitless experience of the self of the previous stage.

Realization of self always coincides with strong idealism. Yet it is initially imagined only in terms of new achievements attained in society: youngsters are prepared to go to the ends of the earth for their ideals: to fight, and even to die for them. It is only at a much later age they discover there is also an inner path to self-realization, when the will is turned inwards to work upon the self; when education and inner development of the *self* are considered a pre-requisite of the right to act in a revolutionary manner in society.

The way in which self-realization first manifests depends on the way in which self-consciousness and self-experience have gone previously. In other words, the idealism of young girls and boys depends on the relationship they have formed with the world. Consciousness of self, experience of self, realization of self always represent a process of separation from the outer world, every time in a different region of the soul. It is the work of a true teacher to maintain a balance, during these stages, between an excessively strong expression of the youngster's own impulses against other people on the one hand, and the extinction of the personality, which results in a slavish subjugation to other people or to one's own desires, on the other.

If earlier phases have been guided in such a way that the self was experienced as serving a higher and divine world, the child will have felt that even adults recognize a higher authority, and in this way the realization of self can also consist of serving a higher world and working in society with firm individual strength.

The realization of self is man's most sacred task. the most profound and valuable aspects of life are brought out here and given to society. In a higher sense, this is actually a sacrifice. It is best expressed in the words of St Paul, 'Not I, but Christ in me,' for this 'not I' is no denial or extinction of the self, but a fulfilment with a principle higher than the human self, and is the work of a fulfilled self in the world.

It is immediately clear that this view of the self differs from that of a psychology based on psychoanalysis, in which the so-called 'super-ego' is described as the reflection of the commands and prohibitions of parents and other adults. The ego is placed between the 'id' (based on drives) and 'super-ego' (the duties learned in childhood), and arose by breaking away from the 'id'. In psychoanalysis man is seen as consisting exclusively of the lower part of our diagram, and above this there are only the rules imposed by the 'father' (in this case, a human father), and these derive their strength from the threat of castration if they are disobeyed.

The self here described is the active, 'propelling', individualizing force in man's life. As the 'I' develops as a self-consciousness within consciousness, it forms a world-view which is then carried as its very own.

7.4 Consciousness of self: the visual arts

Between the ages of three and six the small child who has come to terms with the consciousness of a self is concerned with building up a picture of his world. As an active being, he wishes to externalize this picture, and therefore the toddler is active and creative in an artistic sense. Drawing, playing with clay and with sand, that is the visual arts in particular, are used as means of expression during this period.

In his drawing the child projects his world image outwards, and that is why these drawings by children are so interesting. An elaborate description of children's drawing would be a book in itself; however, some of the main motifs can be pointed out here. Initially the child, awakening in his head, experiences man as only a head, and will scribble circles or paint a large round shape which is seen as a person. This is followed by a stage when straight lines are added inside the round shape, and later, underneath the shape, when a distinction has been made between the head and the trunk. Finally, the limbs become part of the child's experience and are added. These motifs occur in all the first drawings of three-year-olds. The development of the retarded child could be described as a film in slow motion, when the children remain stuck at each particular stage for months.

For example, a Down's syndrome (mongol) child painted people (representing the Sleeping Beauty and her Prince) as large commas, fat circles with a line underneath, looking rather like tadpoles. In normal children the world-picture develops so rapidly, particularly when there are older brothers and sisters whose drawings can be imitated, that the drawings are soon in the classical style with two circles, one above the other, and rake-like arms and legs.

Besides people, children soon start to draw a house, and then nature with its flowers and tress, or technology, with cars and trains. The fact that they are still so strongly influenced by visual imagery during the first years at school should be used educationally by presenting the material in images and allowing them to do a great deal of painting and drawing. Anyone who can read these drawings has a better understanding of the developing child than can ever be expressed in the marks of a school report.

7.5 *The experience of self. Music and drama*

When the child starts to experience his self at about the age of ten, he enters a new world, that of music and drama. The meeting with self leads to a dramatic experience of relationships with other people, for drama is the conflict between the subjective and objective relationships of the self to the outside world.

It is only at this age that the musical elements of major and minor keys and harmony are really experienced. As small children were productive in the visual arts, the child in this second stage becomes productive in the musical and dramatic arts. The adolescent keeping of a diary is equivalent to drawing by a toddler. The diary demonstrates the development of the self-experience (compare Chapter 5). It starts with the recording of the impressions made upon the self by the outside world and the feeling of loneliness in the world.

The adolescent experiences his self alternately in minor and major modes. He can express his sense of loneliness especially in the minor mode.

Following puberty, those who are artistically gifted feel the need to express themselves poetically. It no longer suffices merely to record the ups and downs of his self-experience; it crystallizes beautifully in youthful poetry, and in consequence the experience of self becomes stronger and more secure. The poetry of youth helps to conclude the process of self-experiencing. Works of great literary merit, are achieved only by very few, but despite failures the desire for this form of expression is common. The same applies to musical compositions. It is rare for young people to have mastered musical form — in this case, musical theory — but more usual to have some mastery of language. This is why diaries are more common than musical compositions.

7.6 Realization of self: social creations

Self-realization is aimed at social life. Now that the child has been an artist in the visual and dramatic arts, he must develop into a socially creative artist.

The life of the child can be seen as a game, one which is a preparation for serious matters. Nevertheless by this stage social activity has become a very serious matter. Our culture is struggling with a solution to the problems of society.

However, the future artistic creation of society can only come about when man has learned the hard way that realization of self does not mean a simple insistence on the individual's own needs, but an education of the self, making demands upon oneself before imposing these on society. The will to give future society a true structure must be based on respect, love and support for its other members.

It is not a Utopian idea to maintain that a first attempt can be made to achieve this in the field of education. But what is above all necessary is to see this self as an individual, not as an abstraction, and this is in direct opposition to the prevailing attitudes.

Since Bacon stated that the child came into the world as a *tabula rasa,* and since Darwinian ideas about

140

the exclusive function of heredity have become popular, man has tended to forget his divine origins. This certainly applies to psychology as a science and to education in practice.

7.7 Schiller's philosophy

In his *Letters on the Aesthetic Education of Man* Schiller explained these problems very clearly. These letters should be better known, for they have become particularly relevant today.

Schiller's psychology is based on the polarity active in the human soul, between *Formtrieb* (the formative, individualizing principle) and *Sachtrieb* or *Stofftrieb* (the natural drives). The *Spieltrieb* (or play impulse) results from an interaction or harmony between these two principles, so that man can be a free, creative agent in the world.

If the *Formtrieb* or formative impulse predominates, it produces a barbarian, who imposes himself forcibly on others as a dictator, while if the *Stofftrieb*, the natural drive, is uppermost we have a savage who destroys everything with his passions. In society people fluctuate between the extremes of dictatorship and revolution. While the too dominant individual violates nature, nature holds sway over the materially-minded man and destroys him.

Every dictatorship will produce a revolution, and every revolution a dictatorship. This is why Schiller, who wrote these letters at the start of the French Revolution, predicted that it would end with an unbridled dictatorship. This man took the stage in the theatre of history a few years later as Napoleon.

Society will be thrown backwards and forwards until the balance between dogmatism and passion is achieved in the individual.

Education must be concentrated on the twofold

141

problem. In any individual the balance can only be found in his creative potential when the self and nature permeate each other to produce something new. The self produces the form, using nature as material for creating a new world, which could not exist without the self, and yet it does not destroy nature, but on the contrary raises it above the level of the purely natural. For Schiller this means that such a creation is also beautiful and artistic. The concepts of art and beauty are given a much wider meaning than usual in speaking about artistic creation.

In this sense one can speak of real 'political' *art*, exercised by people as social artists and of the *art* of education and *art* of medicine. Schiller sees the play of children as a precursor of a truly balanced creation.

Children's play is always an attempt at creation, and therefore always artistic from the child's point of view. This question will be dealt with in greater detail in Chapter 9.

The appearance of the self in thinking, feeling and the will, must lead us to investigate other ways in which the self is manifest in the development of children. Again we shall take Schiller's views as a starting point.

In his eleventh letter, Schiller wrote: 'When abstraction is raised to the highest possible level it arrives at two ultimate concepts where it remains and must admit to its limits. In man it distinguishes that which is permanent and that which is ever- changing. The permanent aspect is the *person*; the changing aspect is the *condition* ... In any permanent state of a person the "circumstances" change; in any change of the circumstances the "person" becomes permanent.'

In the first chapters we emphasized the 'changing condition', while now we are concerned with the 'permanent' person, known as the self. The self accompanies the ever-changing circumstances and contains Schiller's formative impulse, the *Formtrieb*; from birth to death it manifests ever more clearly.

The self as a permanent personality first appears in the way in which the child learns to walk and talk, and the way he begins to use the language of the people around.

As we saw, some children act decisively from the very beginning, others seek support from the environment for as long as possible. In the first case the personality asserts itself at an early age, in the second, the child is carried by circumstance, which sometimes makes him get a move on!

7.8 Drives and restraints on development

In practice, we find that there are two groups of children: first, those impelled forwards by great inner strength, who pass undaunted from one metamorphosis to the next, firmly adopting their position in the world as individuals, and a second group, of children who hesitate before every new metamorphosis, preferring not to undergo it unless they must. Such children, if development is retarded, have a tendency to regress to earlier stages whenever they have the chance or when difficulties crop up.

Thus in practice a distinction may be made between an impulse towards development and a regressive attitude. The one is based on the personality or the self; with the others, a resistance to the various metamorphoses follows from the physical condition and the drives of the individual concerned.

In the normal development these two tendencies are supposed to be in harmony. In practice, one of the two will have the upper hand at any given moment. One might think it would be ideal for the self to seek development as powerfully as possible. However, it is by no means so. For a psychological metamorphosis to take place successfully, the organism must always have reached a particular stage. If this happens too early on, certain functions do appear, but in a less complete form than if they had been delayed, and then they remain stuck at this incomplete stage. Thus an initial head-start incurs a much greater regression later. The old adage that everything should run its natural course remains a golden rule in educational psychology.

A great deal has been written in modern psychopathology about retarded children who may suffer from neuroses at a later stage. This is a well-known, and in most cases children can be helped. If the child is not very active in his development, unfavourable external factors are enough to prevent the normal metamorphoses from taking place. By the removal of such hindrances and by encouraging interest the child can be helped on his way. Of course, if he has absolutely no interest in life, it is a question of abnormal factors, which are not discussed here.

To avoid misunderstanding it should be stated explicitly that reduced activity of the self does not imply anything about its eventual development. It is in fact quite common to find that exceptionally fine and highly gifted individuals, who have contributed to society in important ways, were in no great hurry to develop. They spent a lot of time dreaming away in their safe childhood environment, and with hindsight their biographers may conclude that this afforded them a great deal of protection, so that the personality, awakened at a later stage, had a particular purity and individuality. Obviously such a development, which still lies within normality may yet be very difficult for the person concerned.

Even those who later demonstrate a very strong will,

typical men of action who build up business empires, often exhibit an interest in intellectual matters at a late stage. In many cases a boy who was expelled from school for bad behaviour later has something new to contribute to his culture. Again one has the impression that he conserved his strength so that this could be directed all the more forcefully later on.

By contrast there are others who face life with extraordinary alertness and display a tendency to move on to the next metamorphosis much too early. This is very common among city children today. They are often ready to go to school at five and have already learned the alphabet. During the first years at school they are the clever ones, always with their hands up ready to answer questions; their sharp little eyes see and understand everything that is happening around them. They take home wonderful school reports, but at secondary school, once the education requires deeper insights, they lag behind. They grow up later to be 'pen-pushers' and never become founders and leaders.

The study of such children reveals a particular tragedy. They notice things at a much younger age, which another child will dreamily bypass, and only learn at an age when he is ready to deal with the problem. Thus they have far too much to cope with, and the conflicts in these children may be heart-rending because they are not able to assimilate their problems.

Modern city life, with its chaotic impressions and senseless hurry encourages such precocious development. In addition, many parents — and unfortunately many educational systems — present particular areas of learning to children too early, or too intellectually. The generally accepted argument that the earlier one starts with something, the better it is

145

learned later on, is a totally mistaken line of thought and conflicts with everything that has been found in the field of biological development. A rider knows that if a horse is broken too early, he will have an inferior animal for the rest of its life. So he restrains his impatience and waits for the right moment. Modern man is not as sensible about the most valuable thing in his life: his children.

Of course, it is equally wrong to allow the right moment for learning to pass by. It is generally agreed that for many things there are so-called sensitive periods. If they are missed, it will not be so easy to learn the material at a later age and it will not be learned as thoroughly.

However, in the twentieth century the danger that the environment and the school force metamorphoses too early on is much greater. Therefore it is important to focus attention on this once again.

In fact the precocious child is also disturbed with regard to his physical development. The biological equilibrium is upset, growth is insufficient and the children are pale and nervous, they may be prone to vomiting, lacking in appetite, sleeping badly, and the only cure may be to 'put them out to graze' for six months, until their physical development has a chance to recover.

So much for external factors stimulating excessive development. In some children this fast progress takes place as a result of inner factors. These are the babies who are much more alert than normal children, who do not sleep, drink badly, are easily frightened and vomit, who do not gain weight, but lie awake looking round with frightened eyes. These neuropathic cases are exceptionally difficult as they attain every new developmental stage too quickly. A two-and-a-half-year-old boy stopped gaining weight after the age of one while he moved around like quicksilver, climbing on to everything, touching and fiddling with everything. He was the size of a skinny one-year-old baby and had the face of a wise old man, terrorizing the family and exploiting all the weaknesses present in his environment to assert his will. Obviously this case is not one of normal development, but its extreme nature gives an indication of the trend.

However, the fact that normal children can also become neuropathic has been shown in intellectual families in which both parents have university degrees and the baby spends the first three months in his crib right underneath the TV which is on continuously. When the parents are asked why, they answer: 'She likes it. As soon as we turn it off she starts to cry and as long as we have it on she sleeps really well.'

For a normal development, activity and restraint should be in balance.

Between the two poles of the self and the natural environment human life develops in *time;* the interplay leads to an active equilibrium, and is reflected in the child's play, and in the supreme creations of adults.

According to Schiller: 'Man only plays when he is a man in the full sense of the word and he is only man when he plays.' In his play the child is practising and learning to master and assimilate material in accordance with his inner needs.

A true educationalist is concerned with helping self-realization; for every individual self is a new message from a divine world. The respect for the unfolding human 'I' is the foundation of true educational work, and must be given with love, so that the self can learn to make its imprint on the tough material of daily life.

8. The stages of thinking

The following three chapters will again deal systematically with thinking, feeling and the will.

Thinking takes place in a series of processes in which the world is interiorized. Through active perception, something from the outside world is 'taken in' and transformed into consciousness in the inner world of the self, there is an association with other perceptions which bring about a provisional world-view based on experience.

This transformation is not a specifically human attribute; it also exists in animals. Hunters can tell how an old experienced fox is more difficult to hunt than a young animal. In animals the mysterious complex of forces which we term instinct gives structure to the perceptions, thus strengthening reactions for survival.

Instinct contains great wisdom, though there is an innate complex for each separate species, as characteristic of it as its external appearance.

In an animal the formative, life forces operate, on the one hand, at a physical level where the body is formed, and on the other hand, at a psychological level where the instinct is evoked. The same wisdom is found in both. They are manifestations in different areas of a single 'primal image'.

For this reason everything is more or less automatic. Animal activity is regulated by instinct through needs and drives; in so far as a world picture is formed, experience is at work through needs, within the limits imposed by instinct. This results in Pavlov's 'conditioned reflex'.

Conditioned reflexes can easily be observed in babies, and are present in man just as much as they are in animals. On the other hand, conscious thought is a characteristically human function. In this the content of perceptions is confronted with the self; the self organizes what has been assimilated, and absorbs it as its conscious personal property. Every image is a structure formed by the self, who lives with these images, constantly forming new ones from the old, always active. Certain images disappear from inner sight where they were held, but the self can regenerate them through memory, a renewed interiorization, and in this way observe once more its own production. In fact, the self is so closely connected with this incessant formation of images, and association through memory, that a continuous self-experience is impossible without this constant memory. Consciousness of self and memory are Siamese twins. Loss of memory is accompanied by loss of self-consciousness and self-experience. The fact that it is possible for a person nevertheless to continue to live, floating along on experience and automatically acting 'as a human being', is evident from examples of people who have lost their memory and wander around for months doing all sorts of things before discovering who they are, by which time they are usually in a deplorable condition.

Thus in the development of thinking a distinction should be made between the formation of conditioned reflexes, that is, automatic associations, and thinking in a characteristically human manner.

In babies it is soon apparent how visual and aural impressions, which become perceptions, are connected with the basic drives, and thus become the

150

first reflexes. When he hears the sound of a door opening, the baby expects to be taken out of his cot and fed, and shows his pleasure by contented gurgling. If the expected events do not take place, this may result in a dreadful howling to express displeasure.

The whole field of simple and gradually increasingly complex conditioned reflexes became a favourite area for experimental psychology, and some practioners have gone so far as to acknowledge only this type of association and flatly declare that even later education and learning consist only of the formation of reflexes.

In some ways this view is not incorrect. Almost everything that is learned from infancy up to the loss of the milk teeth is learned by experience that becomes automatic. It is also called habit formation. Upbringing has therefore to make sure that these are good habits. For example, potty training is exclusively concerned with the formation of a useful and good habit. However, after the loss of the milk teeth, and even as an adult, a man acts in daily life by the conditioned reflexes he has learned or acquired. In this sense he is the most intelligent animal in creation. But misguided people even argue that this 'reflex' man is eminently suitable to assume the highest positions of responsibility.

To the extent that man lives by these forces it is possible to predict more or less how he will react in certain circumstances, or what ideas he will have with regard to a particular impression. For many people this side of man produces the ideal citizen or worker.

However, for a complete personality all this is thrown out of gear by an incalculable factor, the individual self, which disregards the automatic process again and again, and forms its own images.

The consciousness of self, which emerges in about the third year, immediately disturbs any simple formation of good habits. This is because during the period of obstinacy the child insists that he wants something other than what habit would expect. The child then starts to form his own images, first sporadically, and then with increasing frequency, building his own world around him and experiencing himself as a king in the middle of his own kingdom.

This is the real period of thinking (seven to nine years).

The first period of thinking brings association of the contents of perception, which breaks away from exclusively physically conditioned reflexes after the age of two to emerge as a psychological function. After the loss of the milk teeth the child enters a period when it builds its own realm of images; in addition, the formation of habits continues at a lower level.

During this second stage the foundation is laid for our existence as true individuals. The self has the opportunity to create its own inner world within a sheltered area, and this can be formed in such a way that individual qualities can be expressed without restraint. Like a king in a fairy-tale kingdom, the self reigns in this little world; all its wishes can be fulfilled, the personal creative forces can develop unhindered, and a period of joyful creativity begins. This developmental stage gives good practice for the creative intelligence that the individual will need later in order to rise above the level of reflex living.

What is assimilated by the child in this stage is experienced deeply; he wishes to identify with everything as intensively as possible so that it can become part of the world of the self. However, there is one difficulty: the outer world of perceptions does not yet reveal itself in its naked reality (this only happens after puberty). The child still needs an intermediary. He is dependent on other and older people for receiving things into his own inner world. He can accept things told him by others but the world itself is still indigestible, and some 'pre-digestion' is necessary during the second stage of life, from seven to fourteen. Adults must offer the child images from the inner world they formed themselves. This can only be done through stories, and in this way the older person offers his own kingdom of the self, thus providing the nourishment needed in this period.

The child cannot use anything that is 'reflex knowledge' in older people, but everything that has been experienced is sucked up like water by a thirsty plant. The above can be summarized: for the child as 'self' the macrocosm is still a closed book, but he can assimilate and digest the human microcosm.

However, the exercise of reflexes during this period is continuing close to — or possibly rather below — the surface of the life of the self emerging in imagery. A proper educational system should take both these aspects of the second stage of life into account.

The correct path would be as follows: first, the child is presented with material so alive and vibrant that he can draw it into his thought-pictures, and his self can relate to it.

Once assimilation has taken place it is a personal experience for life, and the child has a relationship to it. After this the matter can be practised and acquired as a skill to be used automatically.

We shall clarify this with a few examples: reading and writing must be learned as automatic skills. How the should this be taught?

Countless ingenious methods have been worked out for making these skills into reflex action in children in the quickest or best way. Thus it is above all a matter of practice. According to one method, the child systematically learns to make patterns up and down which are then joined together to form letters. In another the letters are immediately presented as entities; still another uses pictures to help with forming the reflex for the image of the letter. Yet another uses an overall approach introducing whole sentences.

The proponents of the various methods are convinced that their own produces the quickest and the best results. However, in all these cases, the result is no more than an automatic reflex. The whole process involves only reflex man, while the real person has remained outside it, bored with all the practice (and tired as a result of boredom).

Using this method an animal with the reflex intelligence of a human being could also be taught to read and write.

However, when the image of the letter is first introduced so that it links up with all the experiences in his story, he will not become bored with the necessary practice and not remain empty and desolate, because his soul is now full of images and experiences.

This can be done in teaching by coupling every letter with an image, so that the 'B', for example, is a bear climbing in a tree to take honey out of a bee's nest. When the child has intensely experienced the story and the images, he paints and draws the bear climbing in the bush. Then it is explained that this bear is called 'B'. For many months B remains the letter of the bear, and while it is practised, the child's spirit is filled with the story and the images formed from it. In this way practice becomes a joy and is less tiring. The child's inner life does not dry up but forms a living basis for healthy spiritual life in the adult.

Learning to write certainly takes longer in this way than in other ways, but the eventual gains are incomparably greater, for in one case the child has only acquired an outward skill, and his inner life has been limited, while in this case, he has acquired the external skill, and at the same time his inner life is enriched.

It is worth taking time, for is it really necessary for a child to learn to write in two or three months? Is there any loss if he only learns to read at the end of a year, if he has gained in other ways? If he has learned to read and write at the end of the first year, he still has several school-years to practise in.

What was said about writing applies to all school subjects, even arithmetic, which is a subject for practice more than any other. The Greeks assigned a qualitative as well as a quantitative value to numbers. To us, five is no more than two plus three. To the Greeks, the number five opened up a different world from the number three. They had perfect and imperfect numbers, friendly and unfriendly numbers.

One may balk at raking up Pythagoras' mystique of numbers, which has been long neglected. However, it is possible that this still contains great educational value for the child. As adults, we do not write business letters in the form of a fairy-tale: 'once upon a time there was a manufacturer who was asked to make thirty thousand dresses, and so on.' Nevertheless, we recognize the educational value of fairy-tales.

The child should be allowed to experience the specific value of the simple numbers. He can learn that the number one is qualitatively different from the number two. He can look for everything that is one on the world: one: alone; two: together. As a child he can experience the moral value of being alone and of being together. One God; man is not alone, but together

155

with God. One lonely person, but where two are truly together, a third is present.

The child may look for phenomena which express themselves in the number four. The four corners of our house, the four points of the compass.

It will be found that the number four relates to earthly things; one, two, and three to moral and divine problems; and five is above all a human figure. Our decimal system is based on the five of the human being, calculating with the five fingers, or with ten on both hands.

In Babylonian times other numerical systems were used which were more cosmically oriented; for example, there was the duo-decimal system, based on the twelve signs of the zodiac, which produced the numerical system with base sixty, which we still use in our twelve hours, sixty minutes and sixty seconds and in the 360 degrees used to divide a circle into angles.

If the child has formed a human and moral relationship to figures, and not yet an abstract scientific relationship, he will again be able to practise with no risk that his inner forces will dry up. He will enjoy some numbers because they are divisible, while others, such as seventeen and nineteen are uninteresting because they are indivisible; in this way practise again becomes fun.

With the arrival of puberty, and even earlier, the nature of thinking changes once again. The protected world of the child's own imagery, where the self can wander at will, is disturbed by the contact with 'reality'. So-called reality penetrates during the critical phase from the age of ten, throwing the inner world of the self into disarray.

If the self is strong in using imagery, it will be able to cope with this assault, and learn to deal with the problems of so-called reality. It will be able to look at them and assimilate them in a personal way, and so arrive at the original ideas which are desperately needed in our culture.

However, if active imagination has withered, the self will not be able to act decisively now, and must fall back on accepting and reproducing the views and opinions presented to it.

In this way the originality of thinking suffers, while the person concerned may be exceptionally 'intelligent'. Some years ago a great Dutch scholar stated that: 'We no longer have potential professors, but only clever assistants.'

During the years following puberty the child's thinking should be guided above all towards an independent approach to problems, again in addition to the practice of skills.

Let me retell a personal experience. When I was at grammar school we had a new teacher for mathematics in the fourth year, an original and singular man who forbade us to learn a single theorem in his lessons of descriptive geometry. He did teach the theorems, but after this we *had to* forget them. Every theorem had to be tackled independently by every pupil; it had to be 'seen', and everyone had to find his own way to construct it. The teacher's motto was that it was better to make a few detours, as long as it was your own work, rather than press on blindly using the theorems. The effect on the class was surprising, and many of the weaker members suddenly became active, while many of the pupils who had been at the top and who had learned by rote, now became merely average. However, the result was that we were all absolutely confident that in our final exams there could be no geometric problem that we would be unable to solve. The teacher insisted that we would all get top marks in the subject and the remainder of our

157

time would be devoted to other areas of mathematics. This man showed us the way to confidence in our own abilities, and many of his pupils still remember him gratefully.

Any lesson, whether it is mathematics or literature, history or chemistry, may consist of exclusively reproducing reflex activities, or may be an exercise of individual abilities. Writing plays, tackling problems with no more than the absolutely essential help are ideal activities at this stage. A few words should be said about some of the educational systems which allow for these activities.

The Dalton and Montessori systems encourage 'individual activity' by the children. For the third stage of development following puberty this is certainly quite acceptable. However, during the second stage, in the first years of the primary school, such methods are extremely questionable, for the reasons outlined above.

Individual activity requires a conscious ability to relate the self to the outside world, and during the second stage of his life the child is not yet able to do this.

Abilities which rightly emerge in puberty are summoned up too early, and a forcing of skills may give an initial head start, but result in falling behind later.

8.1 Memory in education

Modern methods of education mainly centre on memorizing. The necessity for readily available facts imposed by the examination system means that pupils must be able to come up with the required answers at certain times.

Normally the term 'memory' refers to conscious or abstract memory, the ability to bring an image back from the subconscious again to become the focal point of conscious experience. In fact, this is the final form of memory. A survey of memory shows that there are two other more primitive or earlier forms.

The first function of memory consists of the ability which could be called 'localized memory'. This phenomenon emerges in the small child before the development of his self-consciousness.

A child who has once been in a certain place may not yet be able to remember what he did there, but some time later when he returns to the same place, his behaviour reveals that he knows his way around and still knows where certain articles were kept and what was done with them. This phenomenon can be observed time and again in toddlers aged two-and-a-half: for example, a hammer and pliers may have been placed in a certain drawer up in the attic after the toddler had played with them. Weeks or even months later he may return to the same part of the attic and will run to the drawer to show that he wants it opened and will joyfully take out the hammer and pliers to continue the game where he left off, even though he has not seen them in the meantime or mentioned them at all.

Another example is of a toddler who had been taken in a sports car to see his granny. After months of bad weather and illness, his mother drives in the same direction, and at a certain corner, the toddler cries: 'Go to Granny — go to Granny's house'; he still exactly remembers the way.

It often happens that a mother comes to my surgery with a child who seems to be an imbecile, and tells me: 'Of course, Johnny is very backward because he is seven and still doesn't speak or seem to have any ideas. But he can't be a real idiot because we recently went on holiday to where his grandparents live, and where we had not been for three years. When we arrived at the station he uttered cries of joy and pulled us along to take us to his grandparents' house. He remembered the way exactly.'

It is then necessary to explain to the mother that this is not a very great achievement, since it is the most primitive form of memory, and is present in every child up to the age of three.

This localized memory must also be the earliest form phylogenetically. Probably this explains the tendency of primitive cultures to erect memorial stones in places where something special happened, so that the sign of the stones would bring back the memory the event. Such memorial stones can still be found in many places. Sometimes they are gigantic upright stones such as the Celtic menhirs, and later they were artistically carved, like the triumphal arches of the Roman Caesars.

As this localized memory survives in the deep unconscious layers of spiritual life, such phenomena are also familiar to adults. Anyone who has returned to the house or garden of his earliest days will find that strange memories of youth come to the surface, and experience a need to walk around and see whether everything is still there. At a particular corner in the hall a memory related to long-forgotten spot may suddenly come to the fore.

We like - and our children even more so - to return to the same place on holiday, to follow the same paths and relive former happiness. This form of memory is related to something that was done or has happened and belongs with unconscious will; as such it is entirely rooted in the life of instinct and basic drives. When a particular smell can suddenly evoke memories of youth which had been long forgotten this is due to localized memory.

160

Following this memory related to the will, a rhythmic memory develops related to feelings. This comes before the child can remember facts in abstract form. Joyfully he will repeat nursery rhymes, counting rhymes and songs with rhythmic repetition of sounds. Many schoolchildren who know their tables as a rhythmic chant have to go through the whole table before they can answer 'What is four times six?' The peak of rhythmic memory is between the ages of three and four, with creative imagination, which is often expressed in rhythmic activities.

Rhythmic memory is less unconscious than localized memory and takes place on the dreamy waves of feeling.

In the literature of pre-Christian civilizations, there are many examples; bards were capable of tremendous feats of memory. The Indian Vedas and the Babylonian epic of Gilgamesh seem strange to us, for the endless repetition of sentences and invocations seem to swamp the actual story, and modern man soon loses the thread.

During the nineteenth century the existence of the blind singer, Homer, was disputed because it was considered that no man could be capable of committing the whole *Iliad* and *Odyssey* to memory. However, at the same time, the transcription of the Finnish *Kalevala* from the mouths of village singers, showed that a single person was capable of reproducing an enormous amount of material.

These singers relied on what we have called rhythmic memory. The runic singers sat opposite each other on a bench, like knights on horseback, taking each other's hands diagonally and swaying the upper part of the body to and fro in a particular rhythm. When they had fallen into a sort of semi-conscious, dreamlike state, they started to sing the runes to each other in call and response, and neither the singers nor the audience would tire, even when this continued for hours, or even days.

The fact that rhythmic memory is not tiring is one which has not been sufficiently explored by educationalists. In modern European children this kind of memory survives until the age of nine, after which it is submerged in artistic experience, where it forms the basis of musical and poetic creation, and is increasingly replaced by the abstract conscious memory.

The totally conscious memory of abstract facts can only exist once the self-consciousness has emerged, and the two then develop alongside. In the years before the age of six, when awareness is intermittent memory also has an incidental character; only certain events which made a very strong impression can be arbitrarily recalled. The child still depends strongly on localized memory to orientate himself in the world, and on rhythmic memory for games. The transition towards the increasingly important memorizing of abstract facts should be carefully monitored at school. Initially, the rhythmic memory which is closely related to play can be used fruitfully and without fatigue.

After the ninth year, when experience has increased the distance between the self and the world, a tendency emerges for the child to distance himself from his school work and to assimilate it as abstract material, unrelated to his own spirit; an attitude intensified after puberty.

Before the ninth year the child is much more involved with what is presented in school, and identifies with the content. Therefore the teacher has a great responsibility. The same material can be set out in such a way that the artistic element is present in it, or so that it must be abstractly learned. In fact, he can even profit from the remaining localized memory by asking the children to do such things as rhythmically marching the multiplication tables and relating them to the place where they were first learned. In later life there is no disadvantage in linking certain facts with memories of our school class and the happy times we had, provided, of course, that they *were* happy.

If applied consistently, such insights could mean a revolution of educational methods during the first three years in primary school. Through such method involving activity, much effort can be saved and many children who now have great difficulty in memorizing during the first few years would be able to join in happily and successfully, especially the slow, dreamy children who find intellectual work hard. Such children are by no means necessarily backward, as we saw in Chapter 7, and may in fact be special children who quietly take their time over everything.

Precocious children who are ahead of their years have initially no problems with memorizing lessons. They have good marks on their school reports. However, it is educationally sound to force them to rely on the childish rhythmic memory a little while longer. Experience has shown that if a consistent effort is made to do so, they become more childlike and physically healthier.

Enough has been said about ordinary conscious intellectual memory. It is the ability to reproduce an arbitrary content, unrelated to a definite place or rhythm, at any given time.

If abstract memory is developed too early, it weakens the ability to memorize later on; there is a reluctance to tax the memory, the child will prefers a direct perception of the image or word, a tendency which has been exploited very cleverly by some

163

political movements. Since education during the last century virtually always inclined to emphasize the function of memory too early in development, this matter has become important in our culture.

A related question is whether the system of teaching different subjects every hour, and continuing a lesson started one day on the following day, should be used at the primary school. Instead of this, Steiner introduced in his schools the system of block periods. In this system a single subject is taught not just for the first two hours of the morning, but for a number of weeks at a time, to be followed after a few weeks by another subject. In Montessori schools children are also given the opportunity of concentrating on a single subject for long periods of time, but then the choice is up the child himself. If he wishes to stop and do something else, he can do so. However, the block period system used in the Steiner (or Waldorf) Schools goes further, because the teacher decides on the length and time of each project period in the context of the whole curriculum.

The advocates of a divided curriculum argue that the child may be tired after an hour of arithmetic, and is then refreshed by reading and his interest is stimulated by the change. For every child the lessons he enjoys alternate with those he does not. They point out that three weeks of arithmetic or geography must be very tedious for the children. However, we must ask what effect this diversified curriculum has on the child and what demands it makes.

If the usual teaching method is used, based mainly on intellectual memory, the method of alternating subjects is clearly the one to use. However, to reach a deeper spiritual level during the lessons, this method cannot be used, especially if the artistic side of education is to be given a chance.

A child will always need some time before he becomes completely immersed in anything, and it is characteristic of children, and related to the repetitive character of rhythmic memory, that they will want to continue with those things they are involved in. Only then are they able to relate to anything in spiritual depth. It is only then that the feelings and the will are also engaged and the children become productive. Obviously it is not possible to teach a single subject in an intellectual way for hours or for weeks at a stretch — after a few days the children would be quite sick of it. It is necessary to alternate direct teaching with drawing, painting and modelling based on the subject, and writing essays and stories so that learning and expression of the subject are in equilibrium, like breathing in and out. If the teacher is able to achieve this, the child will *live* the subject. What was learned in one week still has an effect the following week. The child gradually starts to feel at home in a certain subject, and when that particular period comes to an end, it is like the end of a short era in his life, or the end of a journey over familiar ground. The subject can then rest for many months before it comes up again.

The advocates of a changing programme will argue that by that time the children will have forgotten everything. This is their greatest fear, because they only see results when the child is able to recall the subject to memory instantly.

However, anyone who has studied the different types of memory will not be afraid of this so-called 'forgetting' of the content of the lessons. In the first place, practice has shown that after about six months, when the same subject comes round for another period, the content of the previous time is soon recalled. After repeating it briefly for a few days, the children can build on this. In the second place, perhaps there is an advantage if the subject disappears temporarily from the upper layers of consciousness, to rest for a while in the deeper levels.

What happens to those things we once knew and have forgotten? Do adults remember everything they once learned, and if they do not does this mean that it is lost? How many of us now remember no mathematics at all and are not able to solve a single algebraic equation, though we one had good marks for this subject? Does this mean that it is all lost?

The answer lies in the secret that the knowledge which has disappeared from our present awareness nevertheless continues to be active in the subconscious, sleeping part of our spiritual lives; there it is transformed into abilities which are fruitful in completely different areas. The mathematics we once learned and have now forgotten is transformed into a capacity for logical thinking, so that we are better able to draw correct conclusions in a particular situation. If this were not the case, we might as well scrap eighty per cent of the lessons, for no more than twenty per cent remains with us.

As a result of periodic teaching the lessons are repeatedly submerged in the subconscious and temporarily forgotten. However, in the interim the process starts of developing new abilities, and these are available during the next period for new lessons.

The modern educational system is certainly geared more towards passing examinations than towards life. The fear that a pupil will not be ready for an exam forces the teacher to make sure that the child is in complete control of all the facts, so that he can regurgitate it all at once at the required time. However, an examination is an extremely poor yardstick for the true usefulness of material in real life, for it tests only an extremely limited function.

Many things will have to change before the exaggerated respect for exam results is reduced to normal proportions, and the system no longer dominates education. Nevertheless, the appeal for other standards is increasingly made, especially in fields concerned with practical work. In the ordinary system what is learned is mainly related to our intellect. In the block period system the child identifies much more closely with the lessons, so that the knowledge belongs to him, and the transforming of lessons into abilities of use in later life can take place more easily.

The block period system has the disadvantage that it does not train children to achieve top marks in the exam rat-race. Children thus taught are unused to the requirements imposed in questions and answers which seem rather senseless to them. If they have to take exams, they need some months to prepare, but results have shown that their performances are not unfavourable, and moreover that their productive work and understanding of the subject are by no means behind that of others with roughly equivalent intellectual abilities. After the exams, the technique can be forgotten by everyone, and life itself will decide on the usefulness of those who have taken them.

9. Stages of feeling: Artistic development

While thinking was described as a function in which the outside world is internalized, and the will as one in which the inner world is externalized, a characteristic of feeling is that it constantly fluctuates between being open and closed to the outside world.

Sympathy means that the soul is open, antipathy that it shuts out the world and rejects it. Feelings swing between sympathy and antipathy, love and hate, laughing and crying; it is a great respiratory process between the spirit and the world, a diastole and systole, subject to its own rhythm.

Feelings form the real core of the soul. The pole closer to the spiritual self lies in thinking, while the pole related to the physical drives is formed by the will. Forces from both areas influence this central core of feeling (see figure below).

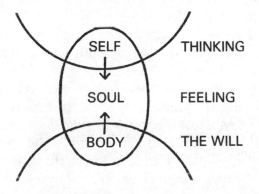

Man experiences his own being primarily in the feeling soul. This is where his deepest human value is determined and this is why the care of feeling is essential to happiness in life and to the individual's worth as a human being.

It is a mistake to imagine that this power will develop spontaneously. A great deal of time and effort is put into cultivating thinking processes, and new paths are being sought to enhance moral strengths. However, all this is worthless if these forces are not bound together in the personality by a healthy and lively capacity for feeling.

Attention to feeling is at least as important as it is to thinking and to the will. While feeling opens to the outside world and assimilates it with positive feeling or sympathy, the whole soul is immersed in the world; it flows out and identifies with it. This can be so intensive as to surrender the individual personality and the boundary of consciousness. In fact, it is not possible to experience identification consciously; this can only occur a moment later when the soul extricates itself from its intermingling with the outer world and withdraws into itself.

The more intensely surrender to the world takes place, and the more intensely the experience is then internalized, the deeper are the feelings and experience a person has of the world. An understanding of this in and out-breathing is the basis for the education of feeling.

This does not mean that children should be encouraged to have only pleasant experiences; if the interplay with the outside world consists only of enjoyment, this will simply stimulate the desire for more pleasure. The important thing is to find the correct physiological balance between pleasure and reflection.

170

Adults know from experience that they have to intervene when children are going too far or getting over-excited.

When telling a story the grown-up is not allowed to stop at the point of greatest tension, but tension should be increased to a climax and then followed by a calming down. If a teacher fails in this, the children will storm out of the class and break down the school.

The same rules which apply for art and drama should be used for this respiratory process. The difference, for example, between dance music and a symphony in this field, is that dance music evokes an ever-increasingly excited surrender, while a symphony is a breathing process of tension and relaxation.

The teacher must compose his lessons in such a way that they are small symphonies or sonatas, with a beginning, a middle and an end. If he does not do this, he will damage the child's health. This should be one of the most important studies of education, and should be practised continually at teacher- training colleges.

The mistake that is usually made is that the child has too little 'sympathy' for the lesson, so that he shuts it out, and the teacher gets the feeling that he is facing a blank wall. In this case the repressed sympathetic forces break out after school in rowdiness. However, if sympathy is summoned in excess or in a one-sided manner, harm comes again. The child may be taken too far out of himself, he no longer knows what to do with himself, and ends up by being destructive.

A good teacher plays his class like an instrument, increasing the tension until everyone is listening with bated breath, and then releases it so that a deep sigh comes from the pupils. In this way he can educate truly harmonious and balanced individuals. This is

171

usually best understood by leaders in youth camps, who are experienced in alternating serious activities and high-spirits.

Possibly this is the right way to take the view now often heard: that school should be more like such a youth camp.

However, this does not mean that school can become a camp and high spirits should be introduced. The contrast between school and camp should continue to exist, allowing a process of breathing in and out, which should be achieved in the school in an artistic way.

In describing feeling in children, a distinction should be made between the feelings themselves and the act of feeling.

Feelings are present immediately on birth. These are the experiences of pleasure and displeasure which appear in relation to the basic drives and needs. Hunger leads to a sense of displeasure; drinking to a pleasure; cold is unpleasant, and a warm embrace is pleasant, and so on. These feelings, arising in reaction to the outer world, to some extent occur automatically. They are also present in animals in the same circumstances.

Feelings in the human sense occur when an enclosed world of feeling has formed and feeling is present as a condition.

Pleasure and displeasure still occur as a result of the basic drives; but they will disappear as soon as their causes do.

Sympathy and antipathy reach further, though they too are only a reaction to the outside world.

Joy and sorrow are human qualities, a condition of the feeling soul; while love and hate require part of the moral personality to enter.

On the one hand, there are feelings which are evoked by drives, on the other, feelings borne by the spiritual self.

The whole range can be seen as the child grows up. The baby has only transient feelings of pleasure and displeasure. The toddler has developed distinct feelings of sympathy and antipathy. By the time he is of school age the child knows joy and sorrow, and in puberty love and hate appear.

The great driving force which brings the child's own inner feeling and then expands is the creative imagination, emerging during the third year of life. By its means the child can close his feeling soul to the world and create his own inner world. Elements from outside are assimilated, but feeling is independent of any direct outer effect.

Living in imagination is how the child learns to experience his feelings. The more nourishment he is given, and the more opportunities he is offered, the greater is the variety of feeling he will experience.

A child needs a sand-pit as much as he needs bread and butter. In this context we may repeat that toys which are only to some extent 'finished', and which can be used for many purposes where a creative imagination will supply the rest, are more valuable to children than toys which are a detailed copy of reality, and where imagination is not called on. In this way games are a 'school for the development of feeling'.

However, during this period it is necessary to introduce a new factor that should be present in nursery schools and during the first three years of primary school.

This is the conscious artistic training which enriches feeling and guides it from the power of the basic drives to a higher level, where spiritual norms give direction.

173

When engaged in building and drawing, the younger child will require some help with building, the older child with drawing and painting to get over the technical difficulties and a sense of what is beautiful or ugly. For this, the child should draw and paint with colours as much as possible. After scribbling with arbitrary colours, he is taught to shade carefully, so that he can make patches of colour which merge together or form shapes. He will also become aware of various qualities of the colours - the warmth of red, the brightness of yellow, the tranquillity of green, the coldness of blue, the inward quality of violet.

At the same time he should be encouraged to observe nature. During autumn walks the colours of the trees are pointed out, and during lessons memory can be strengthened by drawing or painting (with watercolours on wet paper).

The range of feeling can be constantly extended with greater distinctions by telling stories. From the simplest feelings that toddlers have about nice and horrid things, to the glowing love and sense of outrage of the older children.

Very often there is a tendency to concentrate only on positive feelings. This is impossible. It destroys the *drama,* the basic law of feeling. Any attempt to present only positive feeling results in superficial sentimentality.

Feelings are brought forth from contrast and the nature of their polarity. Goethe once stated that man can only experience as much joy as he has experienced sorrow. It is not a matter of guarding children from negative feelings or denying them as such, it is a matter of presenting the feelings as opposites in the correct way.

Every story should be a work of art where not only

the tension and release alternate, but where the love for a noble prince and outrage about the nasty wolf or troll follow each other in a truly dramatic way. When the great and well-known fairy-tales are studied from these points of view, they are seen to be works of art which it is almost impossible to improve upon.

In choosing a fairy-tale the same facts should influence the decision. For example, in a fairy-tale such as Snow White, the respiratory rhythm of good and evil is increased up to the final scene when she is placed in her glass coffin on the mountain and the apotheosis is found in the absolute release by the prince.

Not all fairy tales are equally perfect in their composition. In addition to Grimm's well-known tales there is a good edition of Norwegian folk tales, which also contains many miniature works of art; but also stories which clearly originate from a less pure source. In their entirety they form a valuable resource for the education of our children.

After the age of ten a great change occurs in feeling, as the child more or less leaves behind the primitive world of childhood. Previously he lived mainly in images, now he enters a period of musicality and drama. The light and dark which had appeared from the outside as good and evil, now starts to take part in his own inner life. This process reaches a climax during puberty. It is only then that the world of music fully opens up.

The toddler enjoys a sense of rhythm because this is close to the expression of his will. After this comes his feeling for rhythm and melody. It is only towards the end of the toddler years that a memory develops for melody, first for particular intervals (descending in thirds), later for the pentatonic scale, and later still for the diatonic scale with the tonic as a support.

The child lives in the first simple elements of beat rhythm and melody up to the tenth year. Harmony, the major and the minor keys, are still foreign to him, and are not inwardly experienced.

It is only after the tenth year that the child experiences the light and dark in his own soul, and thus also major and minor in music. Harmony also only becomes an inner experience in pubescence. Therefore in teaching folk music, it is right to begin with singing without harmony and carefully prepare for singing in harmony with canons and rounds.

The dramatic element, which is initially introduced to children from outside by means of stories, becomes inward during puberty. Therefore this is the time for it to be experienced fully, not only as tension and release, as in the past, but as light and dark. Drama can be found above all in history and literature. Characters from history and biographies should come to life for the young person; living people in whose suffering and triumphs they can share.

The children are given the opportunity of expressing these crises and climaxes in the essays and in the plays they make themselves, so that in this way they can rise above them. Again there is a way of presenting these things so that they are profoundly experienced, and totally fill the adolescent's soul. But this is only possible with a block period system which allows time to become wholly immersed in a subject.

A special field of study arises for the artistic development and related feelings of young workers who go to a technical school or have vocational training. Basically these young people have the same needs. However, other ways will have to be found of fulfilling them, by taking into account their level of development and their further vocational training.

It is important then to teach aesthetics as well as the trade concerned. This will influence leisure time later in life, as well as the creation of a beautiful environment. To appreciate good and beautiful handicrafts, rather than cheap, mass-produced objects, it will be necessary to encourage a taste for individually-made products. (Now, years after these words were written, many of the ideas have been put into practice in the introductory classes of technical schools. In technical colleges and in domestic science teaching, a great deal has been done to prepare girls for their future responsibility in the family, and in vocational teaching, for example of subjects like child care and education.)

It is also important to encourage the wish to create a beautiful environment. Furnishing rooms from large choices of furniture which are available for this purpose, learning to arrange flowers so that a single flower against an empty wall stimulates a sense of beauty; garden landscaping and many other subjects fall under this heading. It is only when the taste of the consumers at large changes that better furniture will be made.

The last stage of feeling was discussed in Chapter 6. After puberty, with experience of the duality of light and dark, the inner world and the outer world, and so on, there follows a need for a synthesis of these contrasts. This is revealed chiefly in the search for a religious philosophy. It is strange that outwardly youthful religion may take an anti-religious form. We have lived through a time when young people have become atheists or historical materialists, with

177

religious zeal. For them this was the form in which they synthesized their feelings in relation to the outside world.

Now there is a tendency towards other forms of synthesis in which there is a search for a more spiritual world-view.

10. The development of the will: Morality

In the first chapters it was not explained at length what is meant by will. Yet there is no concept which gives rise to greater confusion. What is termed 'will' by one is termed 'desire' by another; some do not know what to make of it; while it is also common to describe even a baby as being strong-willed.

We shall therefore begin explaining what we mean by placing the will between two extremes. There are many transitional forms, and we shall indicate where it is appropriate to refer to the 'will'.

The will belongs in that part of the human soul where an attempt is made to enter the outside world through activity. The first source of strength stimulating any living organism to activity is the complex of *basic drives*. These operate in the organism as natural forces: as a life force, a force for growth and development, feeding and reproduction. They operate in the subconscious organic life and are present from the first day of life.

In the world of plants growth and development take place without drives. The plant in its course reveals the totality of life-processes. The animal only participates actively in these soul-processes when desires are added to drives. This complex of drives animates the whole animal and is even revealed in external appearance.

Thus, in addition to the basic drives, there are also *animal drives* in animals. Like the vegetative drives, these are also ultimately aimed at the survival of the individual, but they are more complicated, and often seem to take strange forms. The nest building instinct, the herd instinct, the leadership instinct (in a herd), the competitive instinct and the instinct of concealment (which is an organic function in camouflage), and many other animal instincts, serve for the survival of the individual and the species; the instinct to feed relates to the individual while feeding the young includes the next generation.

All these instincts, present in the soul as drives, can also be found in man. The power instinct, the herd instinct, the nest building instinct - all these can be considered as the motivating force behind many human activities. Should these drives and instincts be described as the will? One could point out many other drives which are typically human and do not occur in the animal kingdom. The impulse to stand up, despite the seemingly illogical idea of placing a top heavy mass on a small base; this feat of balance is a typically *human drive;* in addition to standing up, the drive to communicate by means of speech is also a human drive, as well as the drive to represent the world in images. These human drives are distinct from animal drives in that they only develop through imitation in a human environment.

Nevertheless, even such human drives cannot be described as will. The vegetative drives, the animal drives and the human drives, are all produced by forces which are present in the organism itself and arise from it with primeval strength, and are expressed in various activities.

It is only possible to use the term 'will' when these various drives result in conscious activity, interact with the world of conscious experience and are regulated and governed by consciousness. It has been pointed out that this element only starts to appear in the activities of children during the sixth year, when they are ready for school. This is the very first primitive form of the will; it is still ninety per cent drive and ten per cent regulation by insight and experience, but it is now possible to describe this as an incipient will.

Thus drives become will through contact with consciousness. The highest content of consciousness can be considered to be the knowledge of the self as a divine spark and the servant and helper of divine creation. When the consciousness of this wisdom is attained, it regulates the will in the highest degree. Steiner described this highest form of the will as 'moral imagination'.

The whole range of will is represented between games with a particular object and moral imagination. The greater the conscious content of the self in a decision of the will, the more moral this will be.

The will is still primitive when it is almost exclusively based on drives, and is only regulated by coherent thinking when the child is ready for school. It is more mature when the world of imagery has expanded, so that more far-reaching objectives can be set, during puberty.

The will becomes moral when drives are so regulated that a spiritual reality permeates the decision by the self. The will is immoral when the self is consciously suppressed and the intellect is used in the service of natural drives. When the intellect unconsciously serves the drives, this cannot be described as immorality but as amoral. Most of the activities carried out by twentieth century man fall into this category.

Our intellect is used to pursue our drives in a more or less refined way. The result is a culture with many technological aids and a desire for power that does not back down for anything. The will is totally amoral when there is no power to direct the forces of the self into the service of its aims.

One may ask, is it possible to develop the will so far and so highly that drives no longer play a part? It is not possible in ordinary life, as at the moment that basic animal or human drives are no longer present the motivation for behaviour also disappears. In our life on earth we are dependent, as far as the will is concerned, on our own organism and the strength produced by it.

Another misunderstanding, all too common, is the general contempt for drives. Drives in themselves are never bad; they are always aimed at the survival and continuity of the individual and the species. The drive for self-preservation, which is quite justified, exists alongside the drive towards self-sacrifice and surrender, which is an important part, for example, of a mother's love, and is not concerned with the survival of the individual but with the continuation of the next generation.

The possibility of 'evil' occurs when drives enter the realm of the will. All this serves as an introduction to the problem of educating the will and of moral development.

During the first year of life the child is completely dominated by basic drives and his activities are confined to the exercise of organic functions. After this, animal and human drives emerge when the child starts to engage in real play. As his consciousness of self awakens, there is a first possibility of the development of the will. Nevertheless, it does not appear immediately, as the self-awareness initially has little continuity, and the content of consciousness covers only the very first experiences of life.

182

That the child's behaviour is still totally influenced by rhythmic organic processes is clearly expressed in his play. Play is still play for the sake of activity, until the change in the sixth year, when a clearer objective becomes apparent. Then the child is ready to undertake a task which he has set himself. This attitude is a condition for the child's going to school.

At this point the will enters the first stage of its unfolding. The direction it will take now depends on the content of the school-age child's consciousness. Moral development can only take place in this period if the child is given examples which make clear to him a distinction between good and evil. The best are in the form of stories; fairy-tales and made-up stories in which the problems of good and evil are set within his range of imagery. If they are such that he listens in breathless anticipation, and his fantasy keeps busy with them for a long time, they will be most effective. Stories with categorical rules - you mustn't do this, that or the other - will generally have less effect as such warnings remain beyond the child's inner life and are no more than learned responses. This is commonly found in practice when moral development is difficult and a child repeatedly engages in certain behaviour despite numerous warnings.

To give an example: A teacher was asked to treat a choleric boy of eight, who suffered from unbridled tantrums in which he destroyed everything, and whose behaviour generally suggested that he might not be susceptible to moral teaching.

One day he was drawing with a group of other children. The teacher drew a circle on a piece of paper for him to copy. Because of the poor quality of the paper, the pencil went through it and tore it. 'I like that,' said the boy, his mouth distorted in an ugly grimace. Without taking any notice, the teacher turned to the boy's neighbour and started to tell a story: 'Once upon a time a little girl was walking with a doll. A boy came towards her. The girl tripped over a stone and her doll broke. As he passed, the boy gave her a dirty look and growled: "Good, it's broken." But he didn't to see the deep well on the other side of the road and he fell into it.'

For a while all was quiet. The young miscreant assimilated the story in silence, and then asked: 'What did he look like?' 'He had fair hair.' The child apparently felt something here and said, 'I think it's a shame.' 'Do you think it's a shame? Well, stick the tear back together.' Carefully the child taped over the tear and then asked, 'What happened next?' 'The boy called out, "Pull me out — I want to help!" Then when people had come along and got him out and he had mended the doll, the little girl was happy and together they walked on.' After some moments of silence the fair-haired delinquent sighed deeply and went on drawing.

This story illustrates how a teacher needs to deal with a situation with great presence of mind, acting quickly to strike while the iron is hot.

Even if this example, out of context, may sound rather didactic, to say: 'It is nasty of you to be glad when something breaks accidentally' would certainly have left that child unimpressed.

In addition to such stories, made up on the spur of the moment as situations require, there are those with a moral content which are systematically told to children. Steiner advised that the curriculum for the first year at school should contain fairy- tales, during the second year, fables about animals, and during the third year, stories from the Old Testament.

Observing second year children reading and acting out the fables about animals with enormous enjoyment confirms that these have been presented at the right time, and that morality is thus encouraged by constantly enriching and increasing the content of his consciousness.

To say that morality really only begins to appear when the child is ready for school seems to conflict with what was said before: that the first years of life form its foundation. Both aspects are true. A teacher is not presented with a blank page when he starts on the education of the will.

At the beginning of life the seed of the will and morality develops in an entirely different way. The child is still immersed in his period of imitation. The foundation is laid by forming good habits. The child imitates his environment and adopts its habits.

The basis for inner security and a sense of order, as well as the regular and unquestioning performance of duty, is an orderly environment with a fixed pattern of life. Unconscious imitation of word and deed forms the child's later receptivity for conscious moral teaching.

The teacher builds on this imitation. Therefore it is important for him to be familiar with the parental environment if he is to understand his pupils, especially when problems arise. He will then understand which elements are based on imitation of the environment and which on the possible inability to accept morality.

The fact that the influence of the environment through unconscious and semi-conscious imitation does not cease at the age of seven became clear during the last years of the Second World War, when it was shown that moral standards quickly deteriorated and even disappeared because of the example around us.

Imitation, which predominates in the first stage of

the child's life, continues to have an effect in those unconscious layer areas where we remain children.

The experience of self which awakens at the age of ten and reaches a climax in puberty brings inner problems of morality. The adolescent experiences great tension between good and evil, between a sense of sin, penance and absolution. His soul life swings between black and white. Dark drives arise in him, as well as shining idealism. However, for the time being he is not yet capable of achieving a synthesis and accepting both as facts one has to live with. It is particularly when the problem of masturbation leads to internal conflict that this can assume a serious nature and can darken and embitter the adolescent's life for many years.

The only way out of this dualistic attitude is to *do* and achieve something by a decision of the will. It is only with self-realization that there is a possibility of totally conscious moral activity, for which the previous stages, listed below, are a precondition: Firstly, imitating the morality of the environment through habit formation; secondly, learning to understand the problems of life in which morality directs; and thirdly, inner experience of the conflict between good and bad, within the culture in which the child is growing up.

It is only when these three stages of moral; development have taken place and been experienced that the individual has a chance of later having a *free* attitude towards the problems of morality in the world.

If the foundation has not been laid, the individual will obviously have nothing to fall back on later in the ordinary decisions of daily life.

If insufficient material was presented during the second stage, so that the individual's understanding of moral ideas is still primitive, he will be unable later on to make fine moral distinctions.

If he has not experienced the third stage thoroughly enough, moral problems will always remain superficial and sketchy to him.

Conversely, it may be pointed out that continuing to depend on the first stage later produces rigid individuals with automatic reactions, people who judge everything according to standards taken from the environment; they will have the 'advantage' of not experiencing any internal conflict because everything is predetermined for them. However, this is at the cost of an impoverished inner life. They will never achieve the highest moral activity which follows from internal conflict, and was described by Steiner as 'moral imagination'.

Just as often the individual remains fixed at the third stage. He retains the adolescent's inner experience of moral problems without finding any solution. This is revealed in numerous neuroses. They are the cause of many forms of fear, hatred and doubt which are found in life.

The measures to be taken for moral development should be clear from what was said above. During the first stage of life the only course is moral example; during the second stage the child should be presented with sufficient material to learn to understand the problems (fairy-tales and stories, and after the age of ten, many tales from history); and during the third stage a sensible and friendly guidance is required for exploring the depths of moral experiences so that the problems of puberty are viewed in the right perspective.

Finally, in the fourth stage, the need is for individual decision or act. An outsider may give advice, but he cannot help, for the will of a young person, particularly with regard to important matters, can be exercised only by himself since he *alone* is responsible.

10.1 Conscience

The problem of moral development cannot be concluded without a discussion of the function of conscience.

Extremely diverse views are held with regard to the conscience. Modern child psychology is psychoanalytically inclined in so far as it is not exclusively experimental, and conscience is explained as the reflection of parental rules and sanctions, or even as an unconscious memory of our acquired cultural heritage which surfaces in every individual in the inherited traits. Thus the conscience is born from a fear of punishment either by the parents or by the community.

This component undoubtedly affects responses which rise from the subconscious and prevent actions in some situations. To some extent they were assimilated in the first stage of moral development. Like other psychoanalytical views, this is not incorrect, but it is one-sided.

In addition to acquired conscience, formed by unconscious imitation of the environment and *not* by a fear of punishment, there is a deeper side which may be termed the absolute or pure conscience. In the pure conscience a higher knowledge speaks in man.

His self, which has descended from a spiritual world and is enclosed in the prison of earthly existence, is unable to forget his relationship to a higher spiritual order. The voice of this order speaks through conscience. The pure conscience is never concerned with ordinary day-to-day decisions, but with the highest human endeavour. This is Faustian man's eternal problem of returning to the light despite error and sinfulness.

This voice of pure conscience does not speak with the same force in everyone, although it is never entirely absent in anyone who is not spiritually sick. The extraordinary fact emerges that there are moral geniuses, just as there are intellectual, mathematical technical and artistic geniuses. (Erich Neumann calls the renewers of culture and religion 'the heretics of the inner voice'.)

The moral genius does not have to be intellectually gifted in any way, although he must be broad-minded and able to turn his mind to every area of life.

There are children who grow up untainted, even in a corrupt environment, like a lily in a mud-pool, while others tend towards evil, even though they grow up in the most moral environment.

This opens up a profound question for human life - that of destiny. Anyone who is closely involved with such problems will almost despair and accept the idea of predestination, and yet one of the deepest principles of a Christian culture is concerned here, for accepting a given situation does not solve any problems. The important thing is what is done about it. Those who are seemingly not richly endowed should not be condemned, but the spark which must nevertheless be present in them should be kindled, or encouraged to burn.

Often one must be satisfied when despite endless effort and sacrifice the only result is that good and evil have become a problem for the young person concerned. If the Faustian aspect has been awakened and amid all negative events he is not satisfied with a negative attitude, an enormous amount has been achieved.

When working with recidivists it is not usually

possible to achieve much more. From the outside it may seem that all efforts are made in vain, for delinquents return to robbery and prostitution. Yet the inner difference may be very great, and sometimes, after many years, one may hear confessions revealing that the voice of conscience has finally been heard. Perhaps this is sufficient for our life on earth.

Some extraordinary experiences have been recorded in the case of moral geniuses. In one case a completely backward girl, suffering from organic brain damage and epileptic attacks, was a moral genius, even though she said nothing and merely vegetated. In her presence, however, it was impossible to ignore a curious sense of purity and great moral strength. For many years she was nursed in an institution and, repeatedly, sober and unsentimental trainee nurses who came into contact with her would say that in her presence they never had any selfish thoughts and they were inspired to look deeply into themselves. When the girl finally died at the age of eighteen, she lay like a lily untouched by life, like a messenger from another world who had brought deep inner experiences to many people.

The voice of the pure conscience is like an echo rising up from the depths of our soul. The voice calling from the higher spiritual world is always there, but for the echo to be heard something must throw back the voice and make it audible.

This is what determines the strength of the voice and this is why the question of conscience, or at least that of the noticeable effect of it, must be termed a constitutional question. Of course, this is not crudely meant, but in the sense that the forces operating in the body, the soul and the spirit are interwoven in a peculiar way.

It is this view of the nature of the conscience that makes it possible to accept its spiritual constitution as given, and to reinforce morality in the three developmental periods in the right way. By so doing a great deal can still be avoided for which there is no remedy once it has appeared after puberty.

11. Heredity and individualization

Darwinism, which swept the world in the nineteenth century, left a few cuckoo's eggs to be thoughtlessly hatched this century. *The Origin of the Species*, which was written by a scholar at a desk, became the basis of social, political and scientific schools.

The idea of the influence of the environment on the species became a social guideline for historical materialism, which was most consistently reflected in communism and Bolshevism; the excessive importance attributed to heredity became a political guideline for the Nazis; the concept of the origin of man from wandering herds became a scientific guideline for psychoanalysis.

It was certainly not Darwin's intention to generate these movements. Darwin was an upright man living in a generation when people could believe on Sundays that man descended from Adam, who was created by God, while during the week they would write that man was the last link in a chain of natural development under the selective law of the survival of the fittest. However, a materialistic age forgot all about Darwin the Sunday believer, and exalted the weekday Darwin, popularizing his whole theory of evolution in the idea that man is descended from the apes. To this materialist view, man is merely the most highly developed mammal, determined by heredity and environment.

Scientists interested in heredity experimented with plants and animals, and declared without reservation that the results applied to human beings, while those who disliked the idea had no scientific arguments available to contest it.

The results of the practical application of the science of heredity in plants and animals were very successful. Oranges were developed without pips. Threadless French beans appeared, and numerous animals were bred to conform with certain required qualities.

Then one nation declared that it would breed a race with qualities of leadership. The world instinctively rose in opposition to this; the objections that were raised were of an ethical or religious nature, but were rejected as unscientific by those steeped in scientific materialism. The fight against this trend could only be fought with the input of morality and not with the weapons of science. It is only the moral person, the spiritual self, who can serve as the ultimate argument against a one-sided determination by heredity.

A few years before the Second World War a lecture was given in a scientific establishment where tests for training young rats were used as a starting point for certain principles in education. The interesting discussion which followed revealed this could be countered by very few arguments that held water in the context of current scientific ideas, which left man's spirituality out of account.

During the Second World War we have learned that we are not able to do this without relinquishing our humanity, without going down to an animal level, as an intelligent and sophisticated mammal. We have learned that scientific theories can be popularized with terrible consequences.

An external opposition against the social consequences without a rethinking of the initial scientific insights will prove to be fruitless. The same problems will return in a different form, and this concerns *everything that is human:* our nemesis or our survival.

Schiller coined a motto for this conflict: *'Der Mensch ist Vieh* und *Engel!'* Man is beast *and* angel.

We have all had ample opportunity of being presented with the 'beast' in man. It exists in all of us; passions and possibilities which we had never imagined are present in you and me. One thing the war did for us was to show this in all its reality. From the abyss the beast in man arose and threw off its mask.

However, we experienced other things during these years. The 'angel' in us awoke shining, our higher spiritual self, and this self was able to look the beast in the eyes and dominate it. It proved that in the direst need it could be strongest and maintain humanity in circumstances which were subhuman and even 'sub-animal'.

What is the correct place for heredity, and what is the individual mark of man? The answer is generally that in so far as man is an animal, he is subject to the laws of genetics; in so far as he is an individual, other forces unrelated to heredity are operative. The sum total is a compromise in which the separate factors must be identified.

This is important from the theoretical and scientific point of view, as well as in practical educational terms, and therefore for culture in general.

Anyone seeking the factors which unite in this compromise has already taken the first step towards the solution of the problem.

The question of heredity from the above point of view cannot be taken up here, but in general it may be pointed out that there are two fields where the conflict between the individual and heredity may best be observed: in the illnesses of childhood and in abnormal development.

One may attempt to observe to what extent the physical body is suitable for expressing individual forces. It will be found that there are children in whom the tension between the self and heredity is not very great, and there are others in whom it is considerable.

In the former cases a child's development will take place without a crisis, in accordance with the outline given in the first chapters; in the second case development is disrupted by dramatic events.

During the first seven years in particular these will be accompanied by physical symptoms. Later on, especially after puberty, the conflict will take a more psychological form.

The illnesses of childhood are of great importance in the conflict of the self with the instrument given by heredity. Again and again a close observation of psychological development in relation to childhood illnesses reveals that these are milestones in his development.

For example, this is the case if the child catches a common childhood disease such as the measles. The fever, which is part of the disease, causes a high measure of confusion and breakdown of the normal processes of life. Psychologically a child with measles is completely down; he is melancholic, avoids the light, cries a lot and withdraws totally into himself. This state is followed by convalescence when the normal conditions of life are restored and the psychological depression disappears, and is usually replaced by cheerfulness. It is thought that the child is better and can simply go on as before.

However, it is interesting to see what happens psychologically for the first two or three months *after* a bad dose of measles. The child suddenly changes enormously. In a short time his features become more individual, his figure alters a lot and develops much more rapidly than during the year before his illness.

'My child is starting to look more like himself', is the way one mother put it when she saw this happening. It is common to see children who are slightly behind in their development rapidly making up this lost time, and all sorts of regressions reflected in poor toilet training, naughtiness or underdeveloped speech suddenly disappear.

In other words, a bad case of measles is often followed by individualization and progress in the subsequent months. This is understandable when one remembers that there must necessarily be some increased activity of the formative impulse in any convalescence when form or function is restored, and this influences the figure and physiognomy physically as well as psychologically.

It is also interesting to note *when* a child catches one of these childhood illnesses. In most cases, it is simply identified with the source of infection, which can usually be easily found. However, it is good to study those cases in which, for example, one child in a family is not infected by a contagious disease, even though he had plenty of contact with the sick members. He will get the same disease years later when the contact is by no means as easy to identify.

Again these phenomena appear most clearly in retarded children. It is repeatedly found that because of the childhood illness, or perhaps more correctly, following the childhood illness, the child takes a big step forward during his period of convalescence.

In backward children one comes across a whole range of cases in which on one hand the forces of heredity are normal, but the individualization principle is weak, or even entirely absent. In such cases the child initially looks normal but regresses as he gets older and his individualization is increasingly lacking. On the other hand, the forces of heredity are abnormal, but the individualization principle is strongly developed. In this case the child is born deformed or abnormal, but this improves as he gets older and his strong individual will forces him to overcome his handicaps and to achieve unexpected feats.

We can do no more than indicate such problems here. It is only when many people work together to observe such phenomena closely that it will be possible in future to formulate a theory of development, taking into account both heredity and individuality.

The same patter can be observed in relation to sexuality. As a biological 'chrono-typical' development it forces the child to cope with his changing body. If puberty takes place undisturbed, it is physically internalized; and internalized psychologically when the child's own inner world is rediscovered.

In the last century physical maturity has come at a considerably earlier age, and thus it may happen that purely biological sexuality may come upon a child before his personality and psychological development is ready. For a long time it was assumed that psychological development was directly dependent on biological changes. The influence is reciprocal, but there is also a third factor: motivation.

Apart from the developmental process taking place in a natural world, man has also part in a world open to him through his thinking. In this way he makes inward that which remains for the animal an outside world. The outcome of this human process is the creation of culture. Young people discover that 'nature' is a given phenomenon, but that 'culture' is man-made.

By his internalizing, the youngster seeks his own identity, which he wishes to consider as a positive factor in a future culture. This results in a world-orientated view, and temporarily in a motivation geared towards the future.

The initially purely physiological and biological interest in his awakening sexuality now gives place in an individual erotic interest, as described earlier. An individual erotic awareness occurs when there is a relationship, not only with the other sex, but with another person. This other is a different personality and all this is founded in a structure of values and ideas which are part of man-made human culture.

Thus the development of sexuality to a personal experience of eroticism is culturally determined. It is due to the motivation towards the future and the desire to create its own culture that every new generation comes into conflict with the values and customs of the old culture in which it originated.

Changing values, also with regard to sexuality and eroticism, are a positive phenomenon and proof of the third force — personality, every man's individual self.

12. On education and self-education

Everything that was said about education shows that great demands are made on the teacher. In addition to an understanding of his subject, he is required to have some artistic skills, and a strong moral and idealistic view of his profession as such.

A revision of education which is to be a *real* revision, not merely the changing of a few superficial methods, must be expected to take many years.

Teachers will have to have the practical experience which is necessary to expand education further along these lines, and ask *what* subjects should be presented to the child at a particular age and during a particular stage of his development? and *how* should this subject be presented so that all the soul forces — thinking, feeling and the moral will — are evoked?

The Steiner (or Waldorf) Schools have operated on these principles for over half a century, and there is a body of experience which can serve as a foundation.

However, all changes would be worthless if one believed that education should stop the moment a young person enters the world as an adult. Just as we outlined certain stages for the course of the child, there are stages throughout life.

The young person entering the theatre of life at the age of twenty does so with the forces which he has so far attained. His thinking has acquired a certain content, and his feeling has a particular structure which is most clearly revealed in his social and religious philosophy; his will reflects certain ideals which may contain more or less moral substance.

The young adult enters life with a desire to make a 'real' start at last, and the need to experience everything that life has to offer. Following the previous stage between puberty and adulthood, when the world was explored with the help of older people, the young person now feels the need to experience everything independently. This is the time when he wishes to understand the most confused and dark aspects of his own experience in his own terms.

It is a time to accumulate experience in every field of life, by being open to everything without reservations. This stormy period is followed, towards the age of thirty, by a stage when an inner need emerges to step back from immediate experience, to arrange and give it structure, to survey it and assess it in more rational terms. 'Storm and stress' recedes, the inner turmoil calms down and although there is still a strong influence from an intellectual approach, it is possible for the first time for life to attain some equilibrium in tranquillity. Therefore the years from thirty to thirty-five are the most balanced and peaceful years in many people's lives.

However, after the age of thirty-five, and particularly towards the age of forty, a new unrest enters the soul, arising because, consciously or unconsciously, one meets the question: 'From the age of twenty I learned about life by throwing myself into it, and from the age of thirty I consolidated and structured this experience, but what am I going to *do* with this experience now?' What is revealed as inner unrest in the subconscious, is essentially a question concerning the will.

'What shall I do with all this experience?' Of course,

it is possible to live off the 'interest', or do I have a task in the world in which my life-experience can bear fruit. What is this task and where shall I gain the strength to use my experience in a way that will bear fruit?

The fact is clear that this experience of life is of no use in the form of cleverly constructed theories, for the world has enough clever theories to cope with and needs something else. There is a need for experience with which man has struggled and which he has suffered until it is painfully reborn. This pain is the crisis of the years after forty.

Life begins at forty. It is true that in a sense life only becomes reality after the age of forty. Before that time one was preparing, even though after twenty it was preparation for a responsible position in society, where mistakes have inevitable consequences.

A completely new question is raised at this point. What is this? Where does it come from, and how?

The crisis that occurs after forty all too often takes a negative form. Release is sought in external changes when ladies go to the beautician and want to look like their eldest daughter, men start to dress in elegant casual clothes, many marriages reach a critical point, old ties are broken and new ones are formed.

As a rule these diversions are tragic because they do not lead to real inner change. That can only come about with another breakthrough of the self, the spiritual individuality. A new person is born from the spiritual world alone. It is only now that man arrives at his true destination as a denizen of two worlds, the earthly and the spiritual, and finds he is an intermediary between them. Only now can his experience mature to become wisdom.

The storms of this spiritual birth are followed by a tranquil time when the self has the opportunity to grow and mature in its own world. This phase is only completed at the age of sixty, the age of retirement. The individual's immediate social function has come to an end, and the years that fate allows him can mean that he may fully develop his inner life, or it can mean that the ripest fruits are passed on to the culture of his society.

Youth is characterized by three stages, and life itself has three great stages: youth, a stage of development, and finally a stage of spiritual maturity. Each of these three lasts about twenty years, or schematically, twenty-one years.

The need for education does not end with adulthood at the age of twenty-one. The teachers of youth are replaced by others: on the one hand, by life itself, on the other hand, by the individual's own self.

Self-education continues in adulthood by means of an interaction between life and the self. First, life has the upper hand; later it is the turn of the self.

The secret of this continuous process of education and spiritual growth lies in constant search. It does not matter that somebody makes mistakes, it only matters when he continues to make the same ones year after year.

Our society has a dire fear of mistakes and tries to ensure against them in all sorts of ways by means of handbooks and examinations, unaware that in this way it merely hammers home certain mistakes to prevent others being made. For surely no one can believe that an ultimate answer can be found anywhere in the field of education.

We have to carry on between the two extremes: paralysis in the traditional mode, and wild experimentation.

The only real guarantee of a responsible system of education can be found in the sense of responsibility of the individual teacher, his desire to continue to learn from life and by the testing of his actions against his deepest conscience.

A teacher who is not fully involved with self-education cannot really educate children. He could as well be replaced by a video. The modern use of such resources is the result of the general lack of confidence in those who are striving for progress. Nevertheless, an imperfect lesson given by a struggling teacher is of infinitely greater educational value to a child than a technically perfect prerecorded lesson.

Someone endeavouring to move forwards with his deepest moral strength is a shining example, despite his inevitable mistakes, and young people will respect him because they feel that he is related to their own individual growth.

One must have the courage to take certain risks in order to move on. When I was at school I had a teacher who used to say: 'If you don't want to take any risks, you will just have to stay and sit on your chair, and you'll find the leg can still come off the chair and you'll break your neck.'

Taking prudent risks in education means allowing freedom where there is confidence in the knowledge and sincere endeavours of a group of teachers.

Selection of teachers should take place even during their training: only those with great enthusiasm for their subject, some potential for artistic development (which is not the same as artistic talent) and with the will to develop as an individual should be appointed to teach in schools. Those who do not meet these requirements should be encouraged to take up a different direction during their training. This is not the same as rejecting them.

The whole training should change profoundly so that there is an underlying friendship between the teachers and the young an attempt must be made to

205

find the right position in life for everyone. It is only then that we can expect that those who are unsuited to teach will be encouraged to choose another profession at the right time. And it is only then that those with a gift for education can be attracted from other training colleges.

However, in the end the will to educate the self which has developed from a sense of responsibility determines whether the individual *continues* to be a good teacher, for many who start well are overcome by the drudgery.

The fight against monotony is the greatest problem. It is easier to avoid monotony when teachers are able to choose their own methods and are therefore *responsible* for their own activities.

It should not be the task of the state or department of education to remove responsibility from them, for without it a teacher inevitably falls prey to boredom.

Teachers are our immediate future and therefore it should be possible to call upon the best people in society to fulfil this task. They are in a position of trust, and should have people's confidence, also in material backing. If they have this, they will be able to carry out their important task.